I0128943

PERSONALISM AND METAPHYSICS

IS PERSONALISM A FIRST PHILOSOPHY?

Juan Manuel Burgos
Universidad Villanueva, Spain

Translation by Benjamin Wilkinson, SEMV

Philosophy of Personalism

VERNON PRESS

Copyright © 2024 Juan Manuel Burgos.

All rights reserved. No part of this publication may be reproduced, stored in a retrieval system, or transmitted in any form or by any means, electronic, mechanical, photocopying, recording, or otherwise, without the prior permission of Vernon Art and Science Inc.
www.vernonpress.com

In the Americas:
Vernon Press
1000 N West Street, Suite 1200,
Wilmington, Delaware 19801
United States

In the rest of the world:
Vernon Press
C/Sancti Espiritu 17,
Malaga, 29006
Spain

Philosophy of Personalism

Library of Congress Control Number: 2023940491

ISBN: 978-1-64889-921-8

Also available: 978-1-64889-717-7 [Hardback]; 978-1-64889-758-0 [PDF, E-Book]

Product and company names mentioned in this work are the trademarks of their respective owners. While every care has been taken in preparing this work, neither the authors nor Vernon Art and Science Inc. may be held responsible for any loss or damage caused or alleged to be caused directly or indirectly by the information contained in it.

Every effort has been made to trace all copyright holders, but if any have been inadvertently overlooked the publisher will be pleased to include any necessary credits in any subsequent reprint or edition.

Cover design by Vernon Press. Cover image by Bibi Tinsley from Pixabay.

Table of Contents

Introduction

Personalism was born in the twentieth century with the vocation to understand the person as a whole, in his or her complexity and in his or her unity. It was framed within the wide current of the development of philosophical anthropology which had practically just begun, but it did so from a specific understanding of the human being. The human being was unique and unrepeatable, a bodily *who*; he possessed a subjectivity which constituted him as a person; he was free and capable of self-determining himself; affectivity, which reached the spirit through the heart, formed an essential part of his being; he was the result of an interpersonal relationship and he lived in the framework of these type of relationships; he was not only temporal, but biographical and destined for a transcendent end, etc.

These features, and others which could be added, were recognized little by little and not without effort, inasmuch as they were a relevant philosophical novelty, as a powerful contribution to the comprehension of the human being, which contributed elements that either up to that moment had not been recognized, or, although known, were seen with a new depth which illuminated the path of comprehension of the human being.[1]

As these contributions were being consolidated and, to some extent, became common patrimony, other topics began to develop and sought an answer. Was there some type of system or structure – not a closed one, of course – which could give foundation to these anthropological novelties? Were they part of a common vision which could be written, related, and told? Did personalism possess some method of specific knowledge, a way of accessing reality, that

---

[1] Personalism is a broad current with many subcurrents. The main and most widespread, today, is of European origin and fundamentally realistic in character (Wojtyła, Maritain, Von Hildebrand, Stein, Levinas, Zubiri, Marías, Marion, etc.). In addition, there is the Anglo-American current, with initially idealistic characteristics, which has its origin in a certain dependence on German idealism (Bowne, Pringle-Pattison, Brightman, etc.). The author of these pages moves in the field of European realist personalism. Two references that offer a global vision of personalism (European and American) are Juan Manuel Burgos, *An Introduction to Personalism* (Washington, DC: CUA Press, 2018), and J. N. Mortensen, *The Common Good. An introduction to personalism* (Wilmington: Vernon Press, 2017). A specific view of the origins of Anglo-American personalism in J. O. Bengtsson, *The worldview of personalism* (Oxford: Oxford University Press, 2006). A brief comparison between the two in Juan Manuel Burgos, "Anglo-American and European personalism: A dialogue on idealism and realism," *American Catholic Philosophical Quarterly*, vol. 93, n. 3, Summer 2019, 483-495.

could account for its anthropology? Or was it limited to using methods borrowed from other philosophical projects? Could this new anthropology be applied to the areas of knowledge that, in a more or less direct way, are sustained by anthropology, such as psychology, education or bioethics?

The work of personalists in the second half of the twentieth century and the beginning of the twenty-first has attempted to respond to these questions. Personally, I have tried to contribute with the proposal of the method of integral experience, and a systematization of personalist anthropology and of its philosophical keys.[2] But there is still a question pending a satisfactory resolution: *the philosophical scope of personalism* or, in other words, *its position and status in the framework of the whole of philosophy*. It is necessary to establish the ultimate value of the personalist theses and their dependence on or independence from other areas of philosophical knowledge. And this implies, in particular, establishing their dependence on or independence from *metaphysics*, that area of knowledge traditionally considered to be the first and foundational area of all philosophy.

This matter is important, especially if one moves within the broad framework of what is called realist philosophy. This tradition has tended to consider metaphysics as the most radical[3] area of knowledge, on which all the others depend. And, if this were true, we would have as an outcome that *personalism, inasmuch as it is anthropology, would also depend on metaphysics* and, in some way, should also submit to the latter's imperium and rules. First would come metaphysics and then personalism. Personalism would contribute significant anthropological novelties, but it would always be a step behind the foundational area of knowledge *par excellence*: metaphysics. Is this true?

Furthermore, the modern tradition has rejected this way of thinking. For a large portion of philosophy after Descartes, traditional metaphysics has no *raison d'être*, and may be considered as an artificial and abstruse attempt to answer questions that cannot be answered. Thus, traditional metaphysics' answers, and especially those of rationalist metaphysics, would be no more than fallacies that would have to be discarded and left aside, emigrating to the solid and thankful field of anthropology, proximate, accessible, and provable, to the extent that philosophy can be. From this perspective, anthropology – and, therefore, personalism – would possess a rank *as first philosophy*. Does personalism accept this way of seeing things or, on the contrary, does it

---

[2] Juan Manuel Burgos, *Personalist Anthropology: a philosophical guide to life* (Vernon Press: Wilmington, 2022).

[3] [Translator's note: Throughout this work, "radical" is used in its etymological sense. That is, as relating to the roots of something, its most profound and fundamental aspects.]

consider that metaphysics – in a sense that would have to be specified – continues to be necessary and perhaps primary?

These are the questions – difficult but important – that we want to take on in these pages. The philosophical status of personalism is in play, as is the value of metaphysics in a world that no longer seems to accept it. Does one seek, with this rejection, to attack values of which metaphysics would be the final and decisive guardian? Or is it simply that anthropology (and other related sciences) has forced metaphysics into early retirement due to its inability to adapt to the times?

One final consideration. Personalism is a unitary philosophy, but also a diverse one. There are different types of personalism and not all of them are interested in metaphysics, nor would they respond in an identical way to the questions we have just posed. Thus, it is worth the effort to specify that this book is written from a specific personalist position: *Integral Personalism*[4], which is based on the anthropology of Karol Wojtyła, as it is expressed in *Person and Action*, and the contributions of the author of these pages.[5] In contrast to other personalisms, this one claims to be explicitly ontological and to maintain a connection with the classical tradition. And since, for this tradition, metaphysics is the final depository of that vision, it is especially important for this type of personalism to study this relationship and attempt to establish how and to what extent metaphysics is necessary as a foundation for this perspective.

Before beginning, I want to thank Professor Victor Tirado, Dean of the School of Philosophy at the University San Dámaso (Madrid, Spain), for the decisive push he gave to this book by "obligating" me to think once again about these questions on the occasion of the invitation to impart a course in this university in June 2018. I also want to thank the Universidad Popular Autónoma del Estado de Puebla (UPAEP) for having facilitated the ulterior development of the book during my stay at this university in August 2018, in which I imparted the same course. The questions, critiques, suggestions, and commentaries of the participants were of great help to me in rethinking these complex questions and better clarifying the content of this work. In this task, the contributions of professor and friend Jorge Medina were especially gratifying and valuable. Lastly, I would like to thank my friend Benjamin Wilkinson for his effort and dedication in translating another book of mine into English.

---

[4] The denomination Integral Personalism substituted the previous denomination, Modern Ontological Personalism, which was very descriptive of its content, but a little cumbersome.

[5] Karol Wojtyła, *Person and Act and Related Essays* (Washington: Catholic University of America Press, 2021). The connection between Wojtyła and Integral personalism is explained in Juan Manuel Burgos, "Wojtyła's Personalism as Integral Personalism. The future of an Intellectual Project," *Questionaes Disputatae*, vol 9. N. 2 (2019), pp. 91-111.

1

What should we understand
as metaphysics?

These pages can only begin with an attempt to clarify the meaning of the word "metaphysics," the expression under which that content associated with the – more or less vague or precise – idea of ultimate,[1] radical or foundational knowledge or, in other words, first philosophy, have almost always been grouped. That is, knowledge on which, in the end, all other knowledge would depend and, thus, would establish the rules for the basic comprehension of what is real. It is known that Aristotle, unanimously considered the founder of metaphysics, never used this expression, but rather, "first philosophy." And the famous name of his famous book has its origin in the fact that Andronicus of Rhodes, when putting the Aristotelian works in order, placed a group of books that were difficult to systematize after physics (*tà metà tà physikâ*). And this expression, over time, ended up being derived into the word "metaphysics" which was popularized in Scholasticism once the Aristotelian works were received through the Arabs. Despite that very prosaic origin, the term became one of the most honorable and significant names in all philosophy; perhaps, as Marías says, because, "it is not lived out as a prosaic *post-physics*, but as a reverberating, inciting, mysterious *trans-physics*; thus it is, literally, in St. Thomas and, through him, in the entire medieval and modern tradition."[2]

Be that as it may, the term became strongly established in philosophy, aiming at that inciting and mysterious *trans-physics*, that is, what is *beyond* what we see, what is ultimate and, therefore, can be a foundation for everything else. The term metaphysics points to or signifies, since its origin, a special type of knowledge, which goes beyond habitual knowledge and, therefore, would be in a condition to proportion special, more definitive answers. And, in effect, it is so. Metaphysics, since its origin in Aristotle, seeks to respond to a desire embedded in the deepest part of the human heart: to reach a radical and overall knowledge which would explain the world and the most radical enigmas which

---

[1] [Translator's note: Throughout this work, "ultimate" is used as an antonym of "proximate."]

[2] Julián Marías, *Idea de la metafísica* (Madrid: Editorial Columba, 1962), 10. A detailed account of the possible origins and interpretations of this term is to be found in Pierre Aubenque, *El problema del ser en Aristóteles* (Madrid: Escolar y Mayo, 2003).

the human mind is faced with. Is there some structure common to everything that exists? Are there first principles of everything that is real and, if so, what are they? Does a superior or Supreme Being exist? What is matter? What is spirit? What is movement? What is causality? Is there some type of connection between these realities, some hierarchy or order? Is the world finite or infinite, contingent or necessary? Can man reach the truth about these questions?

The questions that metaphysics aspires to answer are as exciting as they are difficult. And, in addition, many of them seem to fall out of the reach of specific areas of knowledge such as ethics or anthropology, which generates, in turn, another complex group of questions. Is metaphysics one area of knowledge or several? Keeping in mind that it addresses topics that are so broad, can it be defined with some precision, or must we limit ourselves to identifying it with a vague and undefined aspiration of the human spirit? Does there exist one, several, or many metaphysics? Did only the scholastics do metaphysics or is the work of great philosophers such as Kant, Hegel, and Husserl also metaphysics? What is its relation with the rest of philosophy? With the social and human sciences? With experimental knowledge? Why have modern and postmodern thought gone against metaphysics?

And that is enough, because the complexity of the topic is more than evident. In fact, the problems posed possess such complexity and relevance that one could reasonably doubt about the possibility of resolving them. But this does not change things: metaphysics exists as a human aspiration and as a historically consolidated type of philosophy, and personalism must define its position with respect to it. And it does not appear that there is another possible path for *initiating* this task than unraveling and containing the problem by specifying *the different meanings of the term metaphysics.* Divide and conquer. Or maybe not. In any case, all the great philosophical terms are polysemic, we might say even excessively polysemic. And only if the meanings embedded within each one are delimited is it possible to proceed to a minimally coherent and significant analysis of the questions in play. Otherwise, the discussions may end up being about misunderstandings which generate diverse interpretations in the minds of the disputers.

Therefore, we are going to propose a classification of the possible meanings of the term metaphysics. In particular, our analysis of the problem has led us to fix four principal meanings: 1) Metaphysics as an overall knowledge about reality, or a worldview; 2) Metaphysics as first philosophy or a radical knowledge which, in turn, can be subdivided into: a) Metaphysics or first philosophy as a knowledge which unveils the structure of what is real (categories, principles, causes) and b) Metaphysics or first philosophy as the epistemologically ultimate area of knowledge; 3) Metaphysics as a philosophy capable of generating Meaning; 4) Metaphysics as metaphysics of being. Properly speaking, the fourth and final one is not a *meaning* of the term metaphysics, but a *concrete type* of metaphysics, but due to its historical importance, its significance for integral personalism and the fact that, on occasion, an explicit identification is made between metaphysics and metaphysics of being, it is worth considering on its own. In fact, we will dedicate the maximum attention to it.

These distinctions seem to us to be decisive in comprehending the multiple contents which may be observed in the term metaphysics, but the clarity, it is evident, will not be complete. On one hand, the meanings are not perfectly discernible, and they overlap and mutually imply one another. But, in addition and above all, the meaning of each one of these definitions depends, in the final instance, on the philosophical vision that one possesses, which, in turn, impacts the meaning of the distinction. Hume, Hegel, Kant, and Thomas Aquinas have very different conceptions of what is ultimate and what is first. But this limitation cannot be overcome.

1.1 Metaphysics as Overall Knowledge about Reality, or Worldview

The first meaning which characterizes metaphysics is that of an overall knowledge or a worldview. Every human being possesses a partial knowledge of many aspects of reality, but it is much more difficult to acquire an overall or general knowledge which can proportion a horizon of ultimate meaning to our existence. And this knowledge is important and necessary since, if we do not frame our partial areas of knowledge within an overall horizon, the aspiration to Meaning, a characteristic peculiar to the human spirit remains unsatisfied and leaves a vacuum that is difficult to fill. In this context, what is expected of metaphysics is that it may proportion some explanation *of everything that exists*. Not about this or that, but about *everything*, about the why behind what exists, its structure, its relations, its hierarchy, its origin, its meaning, its past, its present, and its future.[3]

It is clear that, by setting out these theses, we are asking much of metaphysics, and it is thus that, from this perspective, perhaps it might be more opportune to characterize it as wisdom than as science. It does not seem to be simple for man to achieve science, certain knowledge by causes, of so radical and profound topics as these. And, much less, of all of them. But perhaps it is possible to achieve some type of knowledge, of wisdom, of valid illumination, even if not reducible to syllogistic or argumentative processes. In any case, that knowledge is necessary, and the enterprise of acquiring it, of conquering it, is always going to be present in the mind of man and associated, in one way or

---

[3] Cf. Francisco Suárez, *Disputationes metafísicas*, Disp. I, section 5: "If metaphysics is the most perfect speculative science and true wisdom" (Madrid: Ed. Tecnos, 2011), 76-92.

another, with philosophy. But not with all of philosophy, but only with that philosophy which aspires to overall knowledge of what is real, to generating a worldview. Only such a philosophy will be metaphysics, while the rest of philosophical knowledge will be partial or secondary; important, no doubt, but devoid of a universal and total character.

This first characterization of metaphysics generates, automatically, a consequence that is perhaps unwanted, but inevitable. *It is not possible for only one metaphysics to exist.* There will be as many metaphysics as there are philosophical schools, since each one of them will proportion "its own" overall explanation of reality, that is, its own particular worldview which will comprehend, probably, not just its vision of reality, but its interpretation of what the ultimacy, radicality and globality consist in, as well as the way to know this. In any case, every philosophy with a vocation for ultimacy will have, in one way or another, its own metaphysics; something which does not happen always, since there are philosophies which, by their own decision, limit themselves to one area of reality, such as political philosophy, philosophy of nature or aesthetics. But every philosophy which aspires to an overall interpretation of the world should construct, in one way or another, its own "metaphysics." And this will be so, even if it is an anti-metaphysical philosophy in the most traditional meaning of the word. Even in that case, to the extent that it offers an overall vision of reality – and it should if it has the pretension of ultimacy – it will be a metaphysics. So, Thomas Aquinas, Hume, Kant, Hegel, Nietzsche, Heidegger, Ortega, and Julián Marías or Zubiri, to mention a few names, have, each one of them, their own metaphysics.

For Ortega and Julián Marías, for example, metaphysics consists in *the analysis of human life*, because, for them, this is the radical and primary reality in which *all that is real and existent* is given to me. "The first thing, therefore, that philosophy is to do," Ortega tells us, "is to define that datum, to define what 'my life,' 'our life,' the life of each one, is. Living is the radical mode of being: I find every other thing and mode of being in my life within it, as a detail of it and referred to it. In my life all else is, and all else is what it may be for my life, all else is what it may be inasmuch as it is lived. The most abstruse mathematical equation, the most solemn and abstract concept of philosophy, the Universe itself, God Himself, are things that I find in my life, they are things that I live. And their radical and primary being is, therefore, that fact of being lived by me."[4] And for that reason, Marías continues, "the theory of human life is not a preparation or propaedeutics for metaphysics, nor a foundation for metaphysics;

---

[4] José Ortega y Gasset, *¿Qué es filosofía?* (Madrid: Espasa, 2012), 230. English tr. *What is philosophy* (W. W. Norton & Company, 1964).

rather, it is from the start *metaphysics itself,* that is: the search for radical certainty about radical reality."[5]

In summary, the first meaning of metaphysics is an overall knowledge about reality. Now, since human knowledge, and especially philosophical knowledge, is interpretive, it is inevitable that numerous metaphysics exist. Metaphysics of being is one of them. And probably the most important. But there are others. There are anti-metaphysical philosophies that can and should also be considered metaphysics in the sense that we have just indicated. And there are metaphysics of an ontological type which are different from the Thomistic metaphysics of being, such as the theory of human life proposed by Ortega and continued by Marías, the metaphysics of Heidegger or of Zubiri.

1.2 Metaphysics as First Philosophy or a Radical Area of Knowledge

The second meaning of the term metaphysics implies the idea of ultimacy or radicality, which is, certainly, another of the essential features of the metaphysical knowledge. This knowledge does not just intend (in the majority of cases) to proportion a worldview, but also an ultimate and radical knowledge. These are two aspects which are very much linked to one another, but not exactly identical. One may, for example, proportion valuable indications about the horizon of the ultimate meaning of reality, but whose level of certainty – their epistemological substance – may be weak or limited. And it is possible, on the contrary, to affirm, with total epistemological certainty, theses like the principle of non-contradiction, even though this principle does not collaborate decisively in the creation of a horizon of Meaning.

This radical character of metaphysical knowledge, perhaps more than its universal or overall character, is the one that characterizes the Aristotelian enterprise of the *Metaphysics*, with its well-known beginning: "all men by nature desire to know." And yes, all men certainly do desire to know, but Aristotle does not allude with this expression to any type of knowledge, but to a very special knowledge; to the knowledge *par excellence* or wisdom, to the knowledge that the wisest and more profound men desire to achieve, to first and also ultimate philosophy. Thus, "it is clear that theoretical wisdom is scientific knowledge of certain sorts of starting-points and causes,"[6] that is, it seeks to know in depth and through reasons. It does not seek mere data, information. Nor is any starting point or principle enough for it; rather, it is

---

[5] Marías, *Idea de la metafísica*, 39.

[6] Aristotle, *Metaphysics*, I, 982 a 1. [Translator's note: Except where otherwise indicated, throughout the present work we will use the English translation of Aristotle's *Metaphysics* by C. D. C. Reeve (Cambridge: Hackett Publishing Company, Inc., 2016).]

principally interested in ultimate principles, because thus it acquires the ability to justify and give an accounting for the other sciences, which transforms it into "the only free science, since it alone is for its own sake."[7] And, therefore, "this science alone is divine."[8]

Metaphysics is, from this new perspective, an *ultimate* area of knowledge, because there cannot be any other area of knowledge to which one may refer to justify his theses. In other words, beyond this area of knowledge, there is nothing, and if there were, that would be the authentic metaphysics. It is the final rung in human wisdom. If it is not possible to know or justify the fundamental questions of the human spirit through it, it is not possible to do so in any other way, since the person does not possess any other deeper cognitive paths. It is thus a *radical* area of knowledge, since ultimacy and radicality are, in this context, equivalent. A knowledge is radical when it analyzes its premises, postulates, and knowledge with the greatest possible depth and critical mentality. And this is only doable if it is an ultimate knowledge, beyond which it is not possible to go: a *non plus ultra*. If there were a beyond, radicality would correspond to that knowledge, exactly the knowledge that has the character of ultimacy. Curiously, this also means that it is the *first knowledge*, because whoever proportions the last foundations, the last explanations, also proportions the principles, the methods, paths, and notions which sustain the philosophical edifice. The ultimate and radical knowledge is also the first knowledge or first philosophy, a denomination which we do find in Aristotelian metaphysics and which we are going to employ to formally describe our second meaning of metaphysics. A meaning which splits into two aspects. One, structural, which points toward its ultimate character. And another, epistemological, which points toward its character as radical knowledge. From both points of view, metaphysics presents itself as first philosophy.

a) Metaphysics or First Philosophy as a Knowledge which Unveils the Structure of Reality

The first meaning of metaphysics understood as first philosophy may be defined as *structural* and appears in all of those metaphysics which consider themselves capable of knowing and expressing the ultimate structures of reality. It is the case of Aristotle's metaphysics, which proportions the categories, first principles, and causes that are present in all that is real. And it

---

[7] Aristotle, *Metaphysics*, I, 982 b 26.

[8] Aristotle, *Metaphysics*, I, 983a 5.

is also the case of the rationalistic deductive metaphysics, like those of Wolff.[9] According to these metaphysics, it is possible to discover principles common to all that is real: ontological principles, like the structures of the real or of the *ens*[10]; gnoseological principles necessarily present in all knowledge such as the principle of non-contradiction or of sufficient reason; and causal principles or, in other words, a universal structuring of causality which should be active in every process and which, for Aristotle, is manifest in his well-known theory of the four causes: material, efficient, formal, and final. A metaphysics capable of proportioning this knowledge of reality is, in all justice, a first philosophy because it is automatically constituted as the starting point of *all knowledge*, by proportioning the ultimate elements (or the first ones, depending on how you look at it) of the constitution and comprehension of what is real.

And, by possessing that content, it also becomes the *regulator* of the other sciences, including the philosophical ones which only have at their disposition partial knowledge, while metaphysics possesses the ultimate configurating elements of reality and of knowledge. Thus, metaphysics is situated hierarchically above other sciences, it is "the most ruling of the sciences—that is, the one that

---

[9] Wolff's position is inspired by Scholastic metaphysics through Suárez, but it insists on rationalization, systematization, and formalization. A position, furthermore, which was perfectly conscious, with which Wolff intended to overcome the Scholastic "confusions and inexactitudes." "Qui philosophiam primam methodo scientifica pertractat, atque adeo philosophica; is non utitur terminis nisi accurate definitione explicatis; nec principiis nisi sufficienter probatis, nec admittit propositiones, nisi accurate determinatas et ex principiis sufficienter probatis legitime deductas, consequenter cum terminos ad notiones completas ad determinatas, adeoque distinctas, tum propositiones ad notiones possibiles, easque determinatas revocat. Quoniam vero Scholastici in philosophia utuntur terminis male definitis, notionibus plerumque confuses, subinde prorsus obscuris, contenti, nec principia sufficienter probant sed in canonibus vagis atque adeo multae exceptionis obnoxiis acquiescunt...." Christian Wolff, *Philosophia prima sive ontologia methodo scientifica pertractata, qua omnis coghnitionis humane principia continentur*, Veronae, MDCCXXXVI, Typis Dionysii Ramanzini Bibliopolae apud S. Thoman, parr. 7, p. 2. It is well-known, in any case, that this excessive rationalism was taken up by the first representatives of neo-Thomism at the end of the nineteenth and beginning of the twentieth century; and it only disappeared little by little until neo-Thomism returned to the more genuinely Thomistic, and therefore less rationalistic, position, characteristic of the great neo-Thomists such as Maritain, Gilson or Fabro.

[10] [Translator's note: Throughout this work, in place of the Spanish word *ente* we will use the Latin term *ens* (plural *entes*). We find no satisfactory English translation of this term. A common translation, "entity," seems particularly inadequate in the context of the present study since "entity" is an abstract noun, while the present work underscores the concreteness of "ens."]

is ruling rather than subordinate,"[11] while the subordinate science can only be constituted as a second science, dependent on that principal science. The degree and modality of the dependence will be subject to each concrete metaphysics and, in the case of Aristotle's metaphysics, it is an ample but not absolute independence.[12]

b) Metaphysics or First Philosophy as the Epistemologically Ultimate Knowledge

However, a significant part of philosophical modernity has fled from this universalistic or primordial vision of metaphysics, considering it inexistent, artificial, or simply inaccessible, but it has retained part of that primary and radical character, just *limiting it to epistemology*. That is, the possible character of metaphysics as structurally first is rejected or placed in doubt on an ontological level, but a first epistemology is considered possible, capable of founding knowledge in an absolute way, which would make it a metaphysics or first philosophy. What is peculiar and characteristic of this first epistemology is, therefore, the *radicality*, that is, the ability to grasp what exists with the greatest depth and fidelity possible, as well as to eliminate all presuppositions in order to avoid the deformation of the interpretations. The philosophy which proceeds in this way founds the radical beginning of philosophy and, by doing so, founds epistemologically any principle or notion on which knowledge is based or can be based and, therefore, becomes a first philosophy from the epistemological perspective. This is precisely the perspective of phenomenology, whose foundational plan is none other than to become a science without presuppositions and, for that very reason, the foundation for the rest of the areas of knowledge. That is, metaphysics.[13]

In any case, even now, interpretations are inevitably present, affecting, for example, the notion of radicality. And thus, although the search for absolute radicality has a long history which began with Descartes, continued to a great extent with Kant, and was taken up again by Husserl, more recent philosophies,

---

[11] Aristotle, *Metaphysics*, I, 982b 5-6.

[12] This dependence, furthermore, is conceived of within the general metaphysical plan, which does not mean that Aristotle always has it in mind in the strict sense, as occurs in *Ethics* and in *Politics*. The whole of Aristotle's works does not possess a lineal and simple connection.

[13] The character of being a first philosophy of an epistemological type does not automatically lead to a first philosophy of a structural type because it does not follow from the possible establishment of some first epistemological paths that there are ontological principles common to all that is real. Phenomenology, in this sense, advocates from a sectorial analysis of reality, and not a universal one, like Aristotelian metaphysics.

like hermeneutics[14] or personalism, have considered that the total elimination of presuppositions is a *naïve* pretension.[15] It is not possible to place human intelligence at zero. There will always be content which we must count on, with which we must begin, and which, in one way or another, will influence the content to be acquired. It would be more rational, therefore, to advocate for *a possible radicality*, understood not as an impossible total elimination of presuppositions, but as a becoming conscious (always in a limited way) of these presuppositions, of their structure, and of the operativity in the human person. Because, in the end, the radical elimination of presuppositions is not possible *without the elimination of the subject*, which ends up leading, paradoxically, to the subject's hypertrophization, as occurred in Husserlian epistemology.

We already have, in any case, a second way of understanding metaphysics: as a knowledge which proportions the first structure of reality and/or a first or radical epistemological position.

1.3 Metaphysics as Guardian of Meaning or a Philosophy Capable of Proportioning Stable Truths

The third meaning of metaphysics joins – along the lines of the first meaning, that of metaphysics as a worldview – with the human spirit's need to possess true and stable content which can account for existence and allow for the construction of Meaning. And not just meaning in lower case, a micro-meaning, but a deep and significant Meaning, that is, a macro-narrative capable of orienting the biographical existence of persons, a possibility which postmodernity rejects.[16] So, metaphysics, in this third definition, would be constituted by those philosophies capable of proportioning this type of knowledge. And those alone. Not all philosophical traditions consider this to be possible; see, for example, relativism, idealism, or the Heraclitans, each one for different reasons. And thus, it is a definition which is mainly circumscribed to the so-called realist tradition, which understands: 1) that the world in which we live is not a flowing river in which nothing persists; there are permanent nuclei of reality; and 2) they can be truly known because human intelligence possesses

---

[14] Cf. Mauricio Beuchot, *Tratado de hermenéutica analógica. Hacia un nuevo modelo de interpretación* (Mexico: UNAM, 2015).

[15] Cf. Juan Manuel Burgos, *La vía de la experiencia o la salida del laberinto* (Madrid: Rialp, 2018).

[16] "Recourse to grand narratives is excluded." J. F. Lyotard, *La condición posmoderna. Informe sobre el saber* [1979] [12ª ed.] (Cátedra: Madrid 2014, p. 55). English: J. F. Lyotard, *The postmodern condition. A report on knowledge* (Manchester University Press: Manchester, 1984).

that ability. Counting on these two elements, a meaning for personal existence and for the existence of the world can be constructed or sought.

Since the metaphysics of being has traditionally proportioned an important part of this meaning, these two terms have ended up being identified in certain contexts. That is, metaphysics of being would be *the* philosophy capable of proportioning permanent truths on which to construct meaning. Which would imply that critiquing *this* metaphysics would imply questioning in general the possibility of reaching meaning. But this is an incorrect reasoning which is inadvertently founded on a synecdoche. Because metaphysics, in this third sense, *does not remit exclusively to metaphysics of being (although it is not excluded); rather, it remits to every philosophical knowledge capable of proportioning ultimate and stable truths about reality.* This is the third meaning of the term "metaphysics."

Metaphysics, *understood in this way*, is entirely necessary for any human spirit which does not want to land up in nihilism. Or so it seems to us. If nothing is permanent, how or on what shall we find the meaning of our existence beyond our changing emotions of each moment or the also changing social customs? What is valid today, what directs the world today, will no longer do so tomorrow, so its value is merely circumstantial and, therefore, incapable of meriting or demanding life-long commitments. Precisely for that reason, metaphysics, in this third sense, is also necessary for *Christianity*. The Christian message is stable and has a precise content. Christianity's essential truths do not change. Its formulation may improve, as Newman already noted long ago.[17] They may be known with greater depth, with greater richness; they may be formulated in a more precise and adjusted way, but the basic content does not change. Christianity's dogmas (the Trinity, the Incarnation, etc.) cannot be modified because they reflect a revealed truth, given, transmitted, not discovered by the human spirit. Now, if philosophy were not capable of showing that human knowledge is capable of reaching stable truths, either because they did not exist, or because human intelligence did not possess that quality, this edifice would instantly fall. How may we justify the existence of dogmatic truths if human intelligence is incapable of reaching them or if philosophy shows that such truths are impossible? There would only be two options: deny the possibility of dogmas, which would imply denying Christianity itself. Or opt for a fideism which would accept the truth of Revelation without being able to connect it with the human mind, a position that would also destroy Christianity, by leading it to irrationality. That is why it is so important for

---

[17] Cf. John Henry Newman, *Essay on the Development of Christian Doctrine* (1845).

Christianity to count on a philosophy capable of justifying the existence of stable truths (feature 1) and that they can be known by man (feature 2).

This is the philosophy which John Paul II has called a philosophy with a metaphysical reach. "[There is a] need for a philosophy of *genuinely metaphysical* range, capable, that is, of transcending empirical data in order to attain something absolute, ultimate and foundational in its search for truth. This requirement is implicit in sapiential and analytical knowledge alike; and in particular it is a requirement for knowing the moral good, which has its ultimate foundation in the Supreme Good, God himself. Here I do not mean to speak of metaphysics in the sense of a specific school or a particular historical current of thought. I want only to state that reality and truth do transcend the factual and the empirical, and to vindicate the human being's capacity to know this transcendent and metaphysical dimension in a way that is true and certain, albeit imperfect and analogical."[18]

It is worth the effort to analyze this rich text because it seems to us that it summarizes very adequately the principal features that a philosophy of a metaphysical range or metaphysics understood as guardian of meaning, as provider of stable truths, should possess.

1) It should be capable *of transcending empirical data.* Philosophy should go beyond what can be sensed, because what can be sensed does not proportion any stable knowledge, something that has been known since Plato. And, consequently, it does not allow one to reach any truth that does not change essentially over time. Any philosophy that limits itself only to what can be sensed will never be able to have a metaphysical scope. Hume is a good example.

2) It should be capable of *proportioning something (some truth) that is absolute, ultimate, and fundamental.* We have already pointed this out. If philosophy is not able to proportion any knowledge with these features, any *possibility of meaning* disappears, and man becomes lost in the cosmos without the possibility of an orientation that might go beyond what his subjectivity dictates to him in each concrete moment. And subjectivity on its own is not only unable to find a transcendent Meaning, nor an ethical order that does not simply coincide with the subject's interests.

3) Both characteristics require the person, in turn, *to possess the ability to know in a true and certain, although imperfect and analogous, way.*

---

[18] John Paul II, Encyclical *Fides et Ratio*, n. 83. See J. F. Crosby, *The Personalism of John Paul II,* (Steubenville: Hildebrand Press, 2019).

In effect, only if one admits this point are the two previous ones possible. But it is only possible to seriously sustain this thesis if one is in possession of *an epistemological theory* capable of justifying it, since, otherwise, we would be before a desire or aspiration, but not before a justified and substantive philosophical position. That philosophy of a metaphysical scope is capable of justifying the fact that man can know the truth in a sure and stable way does not mean, however, that it has the pretension of possessing the ability to know the truth *in a complete and full way*, because the human being is intrinsically limited, and all that he produces, including the truth, may be improved. That is, all truth acquired by the human spirit is perfectible, *but not entirely modifiable*. This is the decisive point that philosophy of a metaphysical scope contributes and without which all deep meaning becomes inviable. This philosophy will affirm, for example, that man is free. It will sustain that this truth is absolute and not modifiable and, in turn, that we can always go deeper into the comprehension of what it means to be free; that the mystery of freedom is not exhausted, that it is possible to enrich or perfect the notion of freedom. But it will never be licit to deny that freedom, advocating, for example, for a determinism of one type or another. And it will not be licit because this thesis is false. In conclusion, the existence of human freedom is a stable and absolute, but perfectible, truth.

4)   The philosophy capable of sustaining these theses would be, in John Paul II's terminology, a philosophy with a metaphysical range or, in our terminology, a metaphysics understood as a philosophy capable of safeguarding meaning. An affirmation which does not point, either in our case or in John Paul II's, to "a specific school or particular historical current," but to any philosophy capable of generating metaphysical scope; that is, capable of proportioning stable truths about what is real. Because this is the only feature necessary to sustain the rationality of the Christian message. Specific metaphysics have their value, which should not be underappreciated. But none of them is indispensable, because the Christian message transcends philosophy and can live and cohabit – as has, in fact, occurred throughout history – with different philosophies.

If we unite these considerations with those of previous sections, we obtain some suggestive conclusions.

1)   Not every metaphysics as a worldview (first meaning of the term) is a philosophy with metaphysical scope (third meaning). Heraclitus, Hume, and postmodernity have their own metaphysics, that is, their overall

vision of the world; but none of these "metaphysics" has metaphysical scope, because they do not offer a stable or ultimate vision of reality; more still, in many cases they consider such a vision to be unreachable.

2)   There can be, and in fact there are, different philosophies of metaphysical scope. Philosophy of being is one of them. But it is not the only one. Ortegian metaphysics, to which we have already referred, is also a philosophy of metaphysical scope which proportions stable and ultimate truths about reality, in addition to proposing a certain worldview. But Ortega does not follow philosophy of being.

3)   Christianity needs a philosophy of metaphysical scope or a philosophy capable of safeguarding meaning, because, inasmuch as it is a religion that takes on Greek reason, [19] it needs an epistemology capable of sustaining its dogmatic truths on the intelligible plane. By contrast, it does not need a specific metaphysics, since it can find support in any philosophy that contributes to that stability. There is no reason, therefore, to necessarily have recourse to metaphysics of being, although one may legitimately do so, since any philosophy capable of founding a stable meaning can serve, in principle, as an epistemological support, as long as the specific contents of that philosophy are, in addition, compatible with the Christian message.

1.4 Metaphysics as Metaphysics of Being

We will now deal with the fourth meaning of metaphysics, which possesses a different tonality because it does not remit directly to a possible way of understanding metaphysics, but to *one concrete metaphysics*: the metaphysics of being; that is, *the metaphysical proposal elaborated by Aristotle and Thomas Aquinas*. We have decided to give special value to this proposal due to its enormous historical weight and its unique relevance in the context of realist thought. In fact, this weight has become so great that it is not infrequent to *identify* both terms. Metaphysics and metaphysics of being would be one and the same thing. But now we already know that that is an error. Metaphysics of being is *one concrete philosophical proposal*: the way in which Thomas Aquinas, from the starting point of Aristotle, understands the world as an overall and, to some extent, unitary reality. But this proposal is not *the*

---

[19] The specific terms of this "taking on" have been exposed carefully and accurately by Ratzinger, who has signaled, among other things, that in no case is it a reduction of Christianity to rationality.

metaphysics, but a concrete type of metaphysics which, in fact, can be very valid.

What must be understood strictly speaking as metaphysics of being? We will return to this question in greater detail in the next chapter, but we can already anticipate that the standard interpretation considers that it is the proposal that Aquinas elaborates, significantly amplifying Aristotelian metaphysics, as González Álvarez signals: "St. Thomas transcends Aristotelianism without abandoning it. Beyond the Aristotelian level of the substantial act, he will discover the level of the existential act with which he will offer us a considerable advance in the conception of the ens."[20]

Aristotle founds metaphysics in general and classical metaphysics in particular by analyzing the structure of *all of reality in a unitary way from the starting point of the notion of ens*: what is, what there is. Metaphysics is precisely the study of the *ens qua ens* or the ens inasmuch as it is ens; a study which is developed through the ingenious set of notions created by him: substance and accidents, the four types of causality, matter and form, act and potency, etc.

Now, Aristotle, as pre-Christian and thus pre-modern, *does not pose the question of being with all possible radicality*. He does not ask the metaphysical question *par excellence*: why is there being and not, on the contrary, nothingness? And he does not ask it because the pre-Christian World never thought of the possibility of the existence of nothing or of non-existence.[21] That the world might not exist in an absolute way was something that for a Greek made no sense. But for a Christian it did. In fact, that is just what creation affirms and, therefore, as Gilson signals, "the doctrine of creation is called to modify the notion of metaphysics."[22] Before creation only nothingness existed or, more precisely, nothing existed, except God, obviously. For that reason, Thomas Aquinas asks that question which was totally foreign to the Greek

---

[20] Ángel González Álvarez, *Tratado de Metafísica I. Ontología* (2nd ed.) (Madrid: Gredos, 1967), 73. See also, among many others, Xavier Zubiri, *Los problemas fundamentales de la metafísica occidental* (Madrid: Alianza Editorial, 1994), chapters 1 and 2.

[21] Judaism possessed the idea of creation, but it did not venture onto the path of philosophy, or, more precisely, it only did so in a very fragmentary way in ancient times.

[22] Étienne Gilson, *El ser y los filósofos* (Pamplona: Eunsa, 2009), 206. English: *Being and some philosophers*, 2nd edition (Pontifical Institute of Mediaeval Studies; Toronto, 1952). "Thomism begins where Aristotelianism ends, inasmuch as, thanks to the concept of creation, it proposes that essence is not the ultimate foundation, but rather, that essence is founded, in turn, on the *esse*, according to a double, radical, and original *Diremtion*." Cornelio Fabro, *Participación y casualidad según Tomás de Aquino* (Pamplona: Eunsa, 2009), 250.

mind, which lived in immanence. Why being and not, on the contrary, nothingness? And he resolves it through the notions *of essence and act of being* in the framework of a theory of participation of a somewhat Platonic character. Every ens, on a first level, previous to the categories, exists, or is, if one prefers, as an act of being limited by an essence that defines it as the concrete being that it is. The entes are on a scale from lesser to greater perfection according to the characteristics of their limiting and defining essences, with the exception of God. Only He does not have a limiting essence or, in other words, his Essence consists simply in Being: He is Pure Act of Being, *Ipsum esse subsistens.*

One may debate to what extent this interpretation is completely precise. One may ask, for example, if one could not find in *Aristotle* a similar perspective, inasmuch as he does not only speak with total clarity about the different meanings of being, but also formulated the existence of a being that is Pure Act. But, although this is true, it seems reasonable to admit – as Gilson, Zubiri, and others have noted – that Aristotle does not pose with Christian radicality the question about being. Therefore, the Pure Act is situated more in a categorial terrain which ends up turning it into a peculiar Unmoved Mover, which is perhaps not even the only one.[23] We are fully conscious, in any case, that it is very difficult, not to say impossible, to establish an uncontestable position on these nuances. And, although we will return to them, we already note that we will take this consolidated position as the starting point, even as we note that an oscillation in the weight of the contribution of Aristotle or of Thomas would not substantially affect the theses that we want to sustain; that is, this question would not substantially affect its relevance for the personalist position and for anthropology.

The fourth meaning of metaphysics, the most well-known one, is, therefore, this one: metaphysics of being in the interpretation that we just set forth. And *the principal objective of these reflections* is to evaluate what is the position that Integral Personalism can or should adopt regarding this type of philosophy. But, in order for this analysis to be performed with all possible radicality and freedom, it is advisable to insist once again on two questions already noted, but which it is worth the effort to return to, due to the enormous mental inertia that such a powerful tradition generates. The first question is whether metaphysics of being *is not the only philosophy with metaphysical scope,* which means that, in case one questions its affirmations, that does not mean that one is questioning the possibility of reaching stable knowledge or the possibility of

---

[23] Cf. Aristotle, *Metaphysics,* Book XII.

Meaning, which would certainly be problematic. *One is only questioning the value of this concrete philosophical position.*[24]

The second question, consequence of the first, is whether metaphysics of being is *one interpretation of reality, not reality.* It is a philosophical proposal which seeks to understand the structure of the world, but it is not an evident proposal, either primarily or pre-theoretically, although someone deeply formed in this perspective would end up making this *identification automatically* and practically unconsciously. It is an interpretation or theory that should be *demonstrated. That things "are" is not something evident,* even if the verb "to be" forms a structural part of the majority of grammars. What is evident is that things are there,[25] that they are given, that they exist. Metaphysics of being is *the concrete way in which Thomas Aquinas understands, interprets, and theorizes this datum.* And, like every philosophical theory, it may be valid, partially valid, or erroneous.

Julián Marías has explained it unsurpassably: "One may not simply begin with being, one must derive it and justify it. Because being is an *interpretation,* of reality, that is, of what 'there is'". [26] Being is not a primary, initial, pre-theoretical concept, but rather a derived and secondary one. The pre-theoretical fact is, simply, the fact that things are given, the datum that the world is there. But the fact that the world "is," or that it is composed of "entes" is a specific way of understanding that fact. Thus, one may not automatically say that metaphysics is the treatise of the ens, or of being, that is, ontology (in the etymological sense of the word: onto-logos), because we would be begging the question: taking for granted what metaphysics consists in; taking for granted that "being" exists and that metaphysics consists precisely in the study of that being or of the ens inasmuch as it is (onto-logos). But this is just what one must demonstrate. And taking it for granted would invalidate taking that philosophy into consideration as a metaphysics, because an essential feature of any metaphysical approach is a radical positioning before reality, which

---

[24] The same occurs *when one strictly identifies natural law with objective morality.* Natural law *is not* morality, it is *one concrete theory* (among other possible ones) which attempts to explain this phenomenon. Thus, to critique the theory of natural law does not necessarily imply questioning the moral order.

[25] [Translator's note: The original Spanish uses the conjugated verb *hay* ("there is" or "there are") thus avoiding the use of *ser* ("to be"). In English, avoidance of "to be" is much more difficult. This difficulty will recur continually over the course of this work.]

[26] Julián Marías, *Idea de la metafísica,* 33. Zubiri, along the same lines, considers that this identification between what there is and being or the ens leads to an "entification" of reality; that is, to a transformation of what there is (a pre-theoretical fact) into entes (secondary theoretical concept).

necessarily implies the justification (not the demonstration) of its principles. It is for this reason that Marías adds, "metaphysics cannot be 'defined' previously by its content, because that automatically invalidates it with respect to its pretension; the only possible definition consists in determining its function, what we demand of it. Every other specification with respect to its content or its structure has to be a thesis internal to metaphysics (…). If metaphysics were ontology, this identity could not be enunciated in the title; rather, it would be an affirmation pertaining to the content of metaphysics which, at a certain point in time, would discover such a presumed identity."[27]

In conclusion, one cannot and should not identify metaphysics (in its different possible meanings) with metaphysics of being because that would imply taking for granted that metaphysics of being is the correct metaphysics and, in addition, that *metaphysics must be ontology* or the treatise on being. For now, we do not seek to take a position in this respect. We only want to express the interpretative character of metaphysics of being, its condition as a secondary, and not a pre-theoretical, affirmation, an inevitable condition for being able to evaluate it as a philosophy, and praise it or criticize it if necessary.[28]

---

[27] Marías, *Idea de la metafísica*, 35.

[28] "One must repair an ambivalence that threatens; if one says, 'the ens is what already was,' one has the impression that one transcends from the current situation and describes in the ens an 'absolute' character; but it is enough to substitute the word 'ens' with its meaning: by saying '*what is* is what already was,' one notes that what is affected by the determination 'already' is not 'is' but 'what'; in other words, reality: *that* which is what already was; that is: I interpret as being, now that I have situated myself in the attitude of knowing, the *same* reality that *was* before arriving at that interpretation." Marías, *Idea de la metafísica*, 34.

2

Essential Features of the
Metaphysics of Being

Having cleared the terrain, now is the moment to move forward and analyze metaphysics of being in detail. We have already indicated the reasons. What we intend to do in these pages is to study the relations between personalism and metaphysics in order to evaluate which of them should be constituted as first philosophy and to what extent. And, since we are moving within the framework of the realist tradition, the investigation of this relation inevitably passes through an analysis of *this type of metaphysics* which is the fundamental and principal one. It was necessary, however, to perform a clarification of meanings so that, having arrived at this moment, the foundations and contexts of the analysis would be precise and there would be no place for misinterpretations or misunderstandings. Now, within the limits of any philosophical analysis, that matter is resolved.

So, what are the particular features of this type of metaphysics? We already know that by metaphysics of being we refer to the metaphysics of Aristotle, enriched with the Thomistic theory of the *actus essendi*. And it seems that the most reasonable way of presenting its characteristics is to have recourse to Aristotle in order to set forth the basic and primary structure of metaphysics, since Thomas Aquinas, on this level, does no more than follow Aristotle's proposal. Later, we will have recourse to Thomas Aquinas in order to set forth his principal contribution to this project: the structuring of reality in the duality of essence-act of being.

The essential features of metaphysics for Aristotle can be described with relative ease since he himself presents them with a certain clarity and sharpness in his great work *Metaphysics*. And we say with a "certain" clarity, because his brilliant expositions, which, on occasion, even adopt a closed syllogistic character, should not deceive one regarding their *complexity* and a certain ambiguity, which have caused innumerable debates, difficult to resolve. This and other difficulties can be attributed to the peculiar character of this book, perhaps not entirely redacted by Aristotle but in part by his disciples or to the fact that its composition in its current form was not the work of Aristotle.[1] But, be that as it may, and since we do not know the history of these works, the Aristotle which exists for us is none other than the Aristotle of his works, and to them we must remit. We do not want, moreover, to enter into a very specialized discussion of a philological type, since that would lead us outside of the objectives of this text, which does not intend to establish with *complete* precision the features of Aristotelian metaphysics, if that were possible,[2] but to analyze the value, weight, and structural relevance of this thought in relation to personalist anthropology.

We move forward, then, to establish the central features of metaphysics of being, relevant to our investigation.

2.1 The Object of Metaphysics

Aristotle founds metaphysics when he indicates that he wants to perform a study which will encompass *all that is real*, all that is, and study it precisely *under this particular feature*: not for being this or that, but simply for being.[3] Metaphysics, in his own words, is "a science that gets a theoretical grasp on *what is qua something that is* [being qua being] and of the [coincidents] belonging intrinsically to it. But this is not the same as any of the so-called special sciences, since none of these investigates *what is qua something that is* [being qua being] in a universal way. Rather, each cuts off a part of being and gets a theoretical grasp on what is an [intrinsic] coincident of that—as, for example, the mathematical sciences do."[4]

---

[1] "The fourteen Aristotelian books traditionally edited under the title *Metaphysics* do not form a unitary and systematic treatise, but a series of independent works, which would have been subsequently grouped together, in part by Aristotle himself and definitively by later Peripatetics, until resulting in the form in which we currently know the *Metaphysics*." Tomás Calvo, Introducción a la *Metafísica* (Gredos, Madrid 2014), 9.

[2] Aubenque proportions a crude description of the problems which the general interpretation of the Aristotelian texts poses (cf. Aubenque, *El problema del ser en Aristóteles*, 9-22). And we find a particular case of these difficulties in the efforts of Groarke to establish the exact meaning of the notion of induction from the starting point of the few texts that exist in this regard and the multiplicity of meanings that Aristotle proposes. Cf. Louis Groarke, *An Aristotelian Account of Induction. Creating Something from Nothing* (Montreal: McGill-Queen's University Press, 2009).

[3] For one who knows in depth Aristotelian metaphysics, the following pages may have an excessively pedagogical character, but it has seemed to us opportune to present them, since much is in play in this exposition.

[4] Aristotle, *Metaphysics*, IV, 1003ª 20-25. [Translator's note: Exceptionally, we have modified Reeve's English translation, substituting "being qua being" for "*what is qua*

This is the well-known Aristotelian definition with which the essence of the metaphysical area of knowledge is founded, and which does not want to occupy itself with what is sectorial and particular, but with *everything* that exists as the *only* way of achieving universal and first knowledge; a knowledge by final causes and principles; that is, a radical and overall explanation of reality. Because, in the Aristotelian mentality, if we occupy ourselves with something sectorial, we will always be in intelligible debt to *the foundations* of that sectorial reality, and our explanations will inevitably be limited; we will certainly know, *but we will not have achieved wisdom,* because we will only have secondary causes and principles, but not the first ones, on which the former depend.

One must note, in any case, in fidelity to Aristotle, that, in reality, the object of metaphysics can be considered *double*, in that it also deals with *the topic of God,* as he himself did in the famous theological book (XII), with its reflections on the Pure Act, the Unmoved Mover, and others. That is, metaphysics would have two central topics: the ens and God, a matter which has generated an enormous debate within metaphysics since it seems to contradict the thematic unity proper to a science. How can metaphysics occupy itself with being in general and at the same time with a specific being – even if it is God – without automatically losing its unitary character as a science? It is a problem of enormous difficulty, the cross of metaphysics according to some, about which many answers have been given, but about which we will not now occupy ourselves in detail.[5] We may indicate, in any case, that the Aristotelian and Thomistic solution attempted to maintain *the unity of this science*, appealing to a causal connection between the ens and God. If God were the cause of the ens

---

something that is." We thus follow the Spanish translation of Aristotle used by the author, which contains important nuances on this point. For clarity, we add Reeve's translation in square brackets, so that the reader can compare. These nuances between translations, however, as the author has confirmed to us, do not affect his conclusions about the metaphysics of being, although they are important if one wants to clarify Aristotle's thought.]

[5] Calvo notes that the principal positions around the debate have been: 1) ontology and theology are irreconcilable (Jaeger, Natorp); 2) absorption of ontology by theology; 3) attempts to articulate the ontological and theological perspective, which would correspond to Aristotle's position: "For Aristotle there is no incompatibility in the fact that ontology is universal, despite the fact that it occupies itself 'above all' and 'so to speak, exclusively' with one type of reality, as long as the latter is the first reality. More still, there is not only no incompatibility, but it must be so necessarily." Calvo, *Introducción a la Metafísica de Aristóteles,* 51. This, in effect, seems to be the authentic position of Aristotle which does not eliminate the fact that it may present problems if it is taken to its final consequences, as has been shown by the onto-theology of Heidegger, which in reality could be considered a fourth possibility: the absorption of theology by ontology.

the duality of objects with the same science could be justified, since, in the end, one would also be dealing with the ens, but under the aspect of its cause and origin. However, especially since Suárez, the option was made for the differentiation, giving rise to ontology as a science distinct from (Aristotelian) metaphysics, which will occupy itself solely and exclusively with the ens, not with God, or, more precisely, it will occupy itself with God only as a determined type of ens. For Suárez, in effect, God "is not the adequate object of metaphysics. God is only, so to speak, the principal object (*objectum principale*). The adequate object of metaphysics is the ens as such, that is, the ens common to God *and* creature, common to the substance and to the other categories. 'God falls under the object of this science' (*Deus cadit sub objectum huius scientiae*, F. Suárez, *Diputationes Metaphysice*, I, 1. 19).'"[6] In this way, metaphysics understood as the science of the ens and of God gives rise to metaphysics understood as ontology, that is, as the exclusive science of the ens.[7]

Another two reflections before continuing. Tomás Calvo's Spanish translation of Aristotle's *Metaphysics* does not affirm that metaphysics is the "science of the ens qua ens," the most well-known and traditional expression, but that it is a science that studies "what is" qua "something that is" [*"lo que es" en tanto que "algo que es"*]. Calvo has decided to use this expression because he understands that in Aristotle there is not an attempt to explain the reality understood as "being"; rather, he intends to explain the characteristics of *what* is (*ón hêi on*), that is, of what there is, of what appears in front of us.[8] This philological decision – whose evaluation corresponds to specialists in Greek – points, in any case, in a direction already noted. Aristotle, as a good Greek, does not pose the question of being in the modern sense; rather, he poses the question about what there is, about what is there as a fact or datum. The question or inclusion of being understood radically as *act of being* had to wait for St. Thomas.

In the same way, it may surprise us that Calvo uses the expression "what is" [*lo que es*] and not the more well-known and habitual of "ens." He justifies that new and relevant decision for similar reasons. Aristotle would never have had the pretension to analyze the *formal* notion of ens (*the* ens), but rather, what there is. But since the notion of ens, especially after rationalistic metaphysics, seems to have acquired a life of its own, being transforming into a formal

---

[6] Pierre Aubenque, *Suárez y el advenimiento del concepto de ente*, "Logos. Anales del Seminario de Metafísica", 48 (2015), 19.

[7] Suárez founds ontology in the sense we have just explained, but not the term, since he will continue using the expression "metaphysics." Cf. Francisco León Florido, *Estudio preliminar de Francisco Suárez, Disputaciones metafísicas* (Madrid: Tecnos, 2011), 38-43: "From Metaphysics to Ontology."

[8] Cf. Calvo, *Introducción a la* Metafísica, 51.

concept (and therefore a problematic one), the best way to avoid that interpretation is to *deconstruct* the expression "ens" in the direction of its original meaning. The ens (*to ón*), in effect, does not mean anything other than what is, what is given, or exists, since grammatically it is the present participle of the verb to be, just as, in the phrase, "the living person," *living* is the present participle of *live* and thus *living person* is equivalent to *the person that lives.* That is why translating "ens" for "that which is" is equivalent to translating "living" for "that which lives." The weight of the philosophical and linguistic translation, however, differentiates the two cases. If we read the expression "living," it is very improbable that we will think of something different from some type of reality that lives. But that does not occur with the ens since this concept has taken on a life of its own, eclipsing its principal meaning. The ens has become capable of remitting to itself, understanding by "ens" something close to "anything in general" and leading one to forget its principal meaning, "that which is," the *concrete* things that are. And precisely to avoid this possible semantic deviation, Calvo has preferred to deconstruct it, putting into focus its primary meaning: that which is, what there is. Which is what Aristotle wanted to study: things that are (that are there), not "entes" as such.

2.2 "Being is spoken of in many ways": the contents of metaphysics

And that which is, the things that are, are numerous and varied. Aristotle, as a great empiricist, is perfectly conscious of this. And, therefore, the affirmation which, in the *Metaphysics*, practically comes right after the definition of wisdom is the recognition that "being is spoken of in many ways," including the "being" which Aristotle now wants to study. Because this being or the things that are, cannot remit to the *concrete* things that populate the world. Wisdom cannot occupy itself with what is diverse *qua* diverse; that is, it cannot occupy itself with birds, fish, or men, because it would be transformed into a concrete science. It must occupy itself with being in general; that is, with the fundamental modes of being in which things are given. Only this study makes sense in the framework of wisdom or metaphysics. Any other consideration leads to a secondary science. A reasoning that leads to the famous Aristotelian meanings of being which we may understand as *the fundamental modes in which things are given or are* and which, therefore, are common to all of reality, or a good portion of it.

There are numerous places in which Aristotle mentions the different meanings of being, a reliable proof of his consciousness of the diversity of what is real.[9] But the place that tends to be considered emblematic is found in the

---

[9] Aristotle does not, however, use the expression analogy of being, more Thomistic in character.

seventh chapter of Book V of the *Metaphysics*, in that kind of philosophical dictionary which Aristotle coined, probably the first in history. And the meanings that Aristotle mentions are these.

1) "Something is said to BE on the one hand coincidentally and on the other intrinsically."[10]

2) "Of things predicated of a thing some signify what it is, some a quality [of it], some a quantity, some a relation, some a doing or a being affected, some a where, some a when."[11]

3) "Further, 'being' (*to einai*) or 'is' (*to estin*) signify that something is true, and 'not to be' (*to mê einai*) that it is not true but rather a falsehood—similarly, in the case of affirmation and denial."[12]

4) "Further, 'is' (*to einai*) and 'being' (*to on*) signify the things we mentioned on the one hand potentially on the other actually."[13]

That is, in this chapter of *Metaphysics*, Aristotle identifies the following fundamental modes of being: substance and accidents; essence and some of the accidents such as quality, quantity, relation, doing and being affected, where and when; being as true and false; act and potency. It is, doubtless, a very rich text, probably the text with the most complete enumeration of the meanings of being, but it has its limits: it is not exhaustive, it is not very structured, and it does not explain in detail what must be understood by each one of these meanings. Therefore, we are going to propose a more structured and explicative list, more in accord with our interests, which does not seek exhaustivity as much as *comprehension* of the principal Aristotelian meanings of being.

a) The Categories

The categories initially arise from the modes of predication, but Aristotle also understands them as modes of being and this is their most profound meaning. More specifically, they are the most general modes of being around which all of reality may be organized: the *supreme genera of "what is,"* which are, moreover, mutually exclusive. One ens cannot belong to two types of categories at the same time. It cannot be substance and accident at the same time, or action and passion. With the categories, therefore, Aristotle constructs his particular

---

[10] Aristotle, *Metaphysics* V, 1017 a9.

[11] Aristotle, *Metaphysics* V, 1017 a25-26.

[12] Aristotle, *Metaphysics* V, 1017 a32.

[13] Aristotle, *Metaphysics* V, 1017 a35, 1017 b1.

worldview, since he comprehensively describes what exists through the identification of the principal modes in which reality is given. And, in this way, he takes a giant step in the construction of his metaphysical project, which precisely aspired to achieve an overall, ultimate, and also unitary knowledge of reality. Here is the Aristotelian genius: everything that exists can be explained, contained, reduced to, or integrated in one of these categories. The world, in the widest sense of this word, is, from this moment on, much more comprehensible.[14]

It is well-known that the principal categories are *substance*, that which is of itself; and *accidents*, that which can only be in another. They are very well-known notions, central in the history of philosophy, which we are going to present here very succinctly. Substance refers to the subject, substrate, or subsisting reality: that which subsists of itself, not in another. And, thus, it gives stability to reality. If there were no substances, this great Aristotelian notion, the world would not be anything but a web of flowing Heraclitan rivers. The fact that this does not occur is the merit of substance, the guardian of stability or, at least, of a certain stability.

The *accidents*, on the contrary, are given in the substance. They inhabit it and, without it, they cannot subsist. And just as the substance is one, although it possesses an analogical character, the accidents are multiple, since they should correspond to the richness of reality. The most extensive and to some extent canonical list of the nine accidents is the following: "Each one of the things that are said to be outside of any combination, either means an entity, or a how much, or a which, or a with respect to something, or a where, or a when, or a being in a position, or a having, or an acting, or a being acted upon."[15]

---

[14] Aubenque indicates that "the Aristotelian doctrine of the categories, more than authorizing a hierarchical and in the end unitary vision of the universe, translates the necessarily fragmentary character of our discourse on being" (Aubenque, *El problema del ser en Aristóteles*, 208). The thesis seems somewhat justified and somewhat forced at the same time. Doubtless, there does not seem to be any rationalistic approach in the elaboration of the categories on Aristotle's part. But it also appears quite clear that he seeks a systematization of reality, since only by systematizing it can one generate a science of being *qua* being. A different question is whether Scholasticism, following that second line, has taken that classification too literally and has canonized it, impeding any development in this respect, and closing the Aristotelian system in order to be able to use it better (cf. ibid., 422). Aubenque insists a lot in the aporetic and open character of Aristotelian philosophy, in its character of searching, but perhaps one must indicate that Aristotle, especially in metaphysics, sought in fact a *system*. A different question is whether he achieved it and, above all, whether that system can be operative today.

[15] Aristotle, *Categories* IV, 1b 25-27. The same list appears in *Topics* 1, 9, 25-27. To them one must add the post-predicamenta, which are understood as properties which follow

Expressions which have typically been translated as substance, quantity, quality, relation, place, time, disposition, habit, action, and passion.

There are, however, other shorter lists, which has caused discussions about what the exact number of categories is, or if there might be some order or priority among them. It is not an easy question to elucidate because Aristotle does not offer motives that justify his lists of accidents; that is, he does not explain why the accidents are these and not others. Nor did he propose a systematic ordering of the categories, something for which Kant would reproach him.[16] But, in a certain sense, these faults of the Aristotelian "system" seem fairly comprehensible if their objective was to reflect the world of what is given, which, as such, has no justification.

In any case, this is the fact of the matter: there are some problems and difficulties around accidents, such as their origin, exact number, and possible justification. Both Olympiodorus, first, and St. Thomas, later, attempted to resolve this latter problem. In Olympiodorus' case, on the basis of the modes of being, and in St. Thomas', on the basis of the modes of predication in accord with the more or less intrinsic character of the accident which is predicated of the substance.[17] And each one, respectively supported by his own argumentative principle, generated the entire list of accidents (a matter perhaps not very complicated if you know what the final result has to be). In another order of things, it has also been noted that the accidents could be classified in two categories: the fundamental ones (quantity, quality, and relation) and the rest of them, which could be considered as derived from or fruits of a combination of the three principal ones, along with substance. All of these considerations have their relevance, especially if one wants to establish Aristotelian thought with precision; but, as we have been bringing to mind, our principal task is to establish *the fundamental meaning of the Aristotelian proposal*. For that, we can accept, without difficulties, the opinion of Clavell and Laborda, who consider that "the *exact* number of categories is not as important, since the nucleus of the doctrine of the categories is not so much the distinction of ten categories, but the distinction between substance and accident and the distinction between some of the accidents."[18]

---

from the nature of the predications (or categories), such as what is opposite, previous and subsequent, simultaneous, movement, and possession. Since Simplicius, it is generally considered that they are not necessary for the study of the categories.

[16] Rogelio Rovira, "¿Una lista desordenada y defectuosa? Consideraciones sobre la crítica de Kant al elenco aristotélico de las categorías", *Anuario Filosófico*, 39/3 (2006), 747-767.

[17] Cf. Thomas Aquinas, *In V. Met.*, 8, and *In III Phys.*

[18] Luis Clavell and Miguel Pérez de Laborda, *Metafísica* (Rome: Edusc, 2006), 91.

b) Trans-Categorial Notions

The categories proportion the last structure of the genera of being. But there are realities, entes, things that are, aspects or dimensions of what exists, that cannot be grouped in categories because they are in many or all of them. They are not exclusive; on the contrary. They are trans-categorial realities or transcendentals. These notions, such as cause or potency, *do not reflect a supreme genus of the ens*, of "what is," of thing, but a feature, quality or characteristic which can be found in *all* the categories, in all the supreme genera of what is, or at least in many of them.

This last nuance leads us to a possible distinction which we are going to use in order to delimit the concepts as much as possible. More concretely, we are going to understand *trans-categorial notions* as those which are present in different categories, although they do not necessarily have to be present in everything that is. And we are going to reserve the name *transcendentals*, in accord with their habitual meaning in the metaphysics of being, for those notions (realities, aspects, dimensions, principles) that are present in any type of reality. This is the case of the one or unity because, as Aristotle indicates, "that the one in a way signifies the same as being is clear from the fact that it follows along with the categories in the same number of ways and from its not being [exclusively] in any category."[19]

We will now present some of the principal trans-categorial notions and, in the next section, we will deal with the transcendentals[20]:

- *Act and potency.* Act and potency, as we have already said, do not remit to specific types of beings but to positionings or modalities of activation of what is, which may be in act and in potency. Therefore, both substances and accidents can be in act or in potency. "To be in act and to be in potency are not modes of being that can be included in the categories. They are transcategorials, because they occur in each of the categories. But this should not lead one to think that they will then be genera of the categories, that is, supreme genera that would be found in different ways in each one of the categories. Act and potency, on one hand, and the categories, on the other, are modes of being that are mutually irreducible and arise from different considerations. In fact, one may say that the categories are the supreme genera. Act

---

[19] Aristotle, *Metaphysics*, X, 1054 a 13-14.

[20] Since we do not intend to present metaphysics in an exhaustive way, some important notions (like matter and form) will not be mentioned or only very collaterally. One could also evaluate whether the post-predicamenta should be included here.

and potency, however, are not genera, because they are not of the order of the essence (the categories, on the contrary, refer to the essence); rather, they are of the order of being."[21]

- *The principles and causes.* Similarly, we may affirm that the first principles and the causes are also trans-categorial. The first principles, like non-contradiction, are active in the entire order of reality. And the trans-categorial character is presented in a manifest way in the Aristotelian mode of understanding causality in accord with his well-known theory of the four causes: material, formal, efficient, and final.[22]

c) The Transcendentals

The theory of the transcendentals was developed systematically in the Middle Ages, but the foundation can already be found in Aristotle, since it derives directly from the nucleus of his system. We may understand these notions as an *amplification and radicalization of the trans-categorials* or, without necessarily passing through these, as qualities, modes of being or specifications of "what is," which are found in *all* of reality. And this is only possible for those qualities, aspects or dimensions of reality which, according to the famous expression, are capable of "converting with the notion of ens."[23]

In fact, we can consider that the transcendental *par excellence* is the ens, or "what is," which, obviously, is in all the categories, and even in the rest of the notions, inasmuch as everything necessarily is or is something that is. Not only substance and accidents are; the causes and act and potency also "are"; and the first principles; and matter and form. Everything is something that is, so the ens or "what is" is the transcendental *par excellence* with a total degree of universality.

The other transcendentals can reach this rank to the extent that they are capable of being "converted" with the ens, an inevitable condition for achieving the same degree of generality. A transcendental, in principle, adds nothing new to the notion of ens, since, in some way, this is impossible. Everything that is – pardon the redundancy – "is" and, thus, is inevitably included in the notion of ens. It is not possible to add anything to what is. The transcendentals, however,

---

[21] Clavell and Pérez de Laborda, *Metafísica*, 143.

[22] In the first book of the *Metaphysics*, Aristotle performs a detailed analysis of the history of philosophy which leads him to conclude that all the types of causes about which previous philosophers have spoken, can be included in the system of four causes that he proposes.

[23] Two classic presentations in Ángel González Álvarez, *Tratado de Metafísica*, 113-170, and Antonio Millán-Puelles, *Fundamentos de filosofía* (10th ed.) (Madrid: Rialp, 1978).

justify their existence by focalizing aspects which, while they are intrinsically included in the *notion* of ens, do not appear in this expression *explicitly enough*. Thus their usefulness.

Aristotle offers this reasoning on dealing with the transcendental about which he speaks the most in an explicit way: *the one*. "Being and one," he affirms, "are the same and one nature, in that they follow along with each other, just as starting-point and cause do, but not in that they are made clear by one account (although it makes no difference if we do take them like that, instead it, in fact, helps with our work). For one human and a human who is and a human are the same thing."[24] The text clearly shows the similarity and the difference between the transcendentals. They are the same, in that they are reduced to or convert the ens, but they do not reflect or manifest the same thing. And, thus, they must be thematized.

Aristotle also notes the existence of two other transcendentals. The first is truth in its ontological sense, since logical truth is only found in the mind. We find the clearest reference in *Metaphysics*, where Aristotle affirms that "as each thing is as regards being, so it is too as regards truth."[25] And the second is the good: "In addition, since the word 'good' is used in as many senses as the word 'being' (since it is said in the category of substance, as God and the intellect; in the category of quality, the virtues; in quantity, the just measure; in that of relation, as what is useful; in that of time, opportunity; in that of place, the habitat; and so on), it is clear that there could be no universal and unique common notion."[26] To these, beauty and, on occasion, *aliquid* or some other, have been traditionally added, although there have been discussions in this respect. Thomas Aquinas, for example, does not consider beauty to be properly a transcendental, but rather he assimilates it to truth and good. And Suárez, in the same way, only names the one, the good, and truth.

The transcendentals present a certain formal aspect, as does, to a certain extent, all of Aristotelian metaphysics, but they reflect aspects of what is real. They are not mere formal elucubrations, but features, structures, or qualities that we can really find in the mystery of what exists. This is the meaning of this text from Hans Urs von Balthasar: "The child is called to consciousness of self by the love and smile of his mother. And in this encounter is the complete horizon of the infinite Being in its totality opened to him, revealing to him four things: 1) that, in love, he is *one* with his mother, even without being his mother; 2) that this love is *good*, and that thus all of Being is good; 3) that this love is *true*

---

[24] Aristotle, *Metaphysics*, IV, 1003b 23-27.

[25] Aristotle, *Metaphysics*, II, 993b 30-31.

[26] Aristotle, *Nicomachean Ethics*, I, 1096a 24ss.

and that, therefore, all of Being is true; 4) that this love gives rise to joy and that, therefore, all of Being is *beautiful*. We add that the epiphany of Being is full of meaning only if, in what appears, we grasp the essence as soon as it manifests itself, if we grasp the thing in itself. The child does not recognize a simple appearance, but the mother in herself."[27]

2.3 The Unity of Metaphysics

Let us now consider the unity of metaphysics, a question that Aristotle addresses directly in different places, because he is perfectly conscious that it presents problems of difficult solution and, since he decidedly defends that unity, he must justify it thoroughly. We will follow his reasoning in Chapter 3 of Book XI.

The problem is this: "Since the philosopher's science is of *what is qua something that is* [being qua being], universally and not of a part, and since things are said to be in many ways and not with reference to one thing, it follows that if they are said to be homonymously and with reference to nothing common, then they do not fall under one science (for there is no genus of such things), whereas if it is with reference to something common, they will fall under one science."[28]

Aristotle is conscious that he is very ahead of his time regarding the characteristics of scientific knowledge. And he understands that this knowledge should have a precise structure in order to be able to explain in depth, by principles and causes, the realities which each determined science addresses, be it mathematics, physics, or biology. And, in order for this to occur, there should be *unity* within science. The physicist is not in condition to resolve mathematical problems, nor can the biologist resolve those of the physicist. Each one is in conditions (perhaps) to resolve the problems of his own science. But since *everything* that exists is so different and diverse, is it possible to achieve thematic unity in some way? Is it possible to find something common?

The Aristotelian response appeals to a certain analogical or similar character of those names. Through the well-known examples of the medical realm and what is healthy, Aristotle shows that these two words can been associated to different terms: a medical operation, a medical explanation, a medical device. Operation, explanation. and device are different realities, but they possess something in common, their relationship with the curing of the human being. Thus, the same name can be applied to them all. And the same thing occurs with the word healthy. We can speak of a healthy man or of a healthy apple,

---

[27] Hans Urs von Balthasar, "Uno sguardo d'insieme sul mio pensiero", *Communio* 105 (1989), 41-42.

[28] Aristotle, *Metaphysics*, XI, 1060b 30-35.

although man and apple are very different realities. So, Aristotle comments, "it is in this way, then, that everything is also said to be. For each of them is said to be because it is an attribute of *what is qua something that is* [being qua being], or a state, disposition, or movement of it, or something else of this sort. And since every being is referred to something that is one and common, each of the contrarieties too will be referred to the primary differentiae and contrarieties of being."[29]

In conclusion, *things are very diverse, but they are; they are something that is.* And, in that measure, they have to be subordinated to first principles, to the rules and categories by which that which is, inasmuch as it is, is organized. Not inasmuch as it is something *determined*, since that would lead us to the *secondary* sciences which study what is particular, but to the fundamental science which studies the general structure of the ens; that is, of any thing which is. One arrives at this consideration, Aristotle adds, through *abstraction*, according to the mode in which mathematics works, which reaches its object, "having first stripped away all the perceptible attributes (for example, weight and lightness, hardness and its contrary, and further, also heat and cold, and the other perceptible contrarieties), and leaves behind only the quantitative and the continuous (sometimes in one, sometimes in two, sometimes in three dimensions)."[30] So, Aristotle continues, "it is the same way, too, where being is concerned. For to get a theoretical grasp on the [intrinsic] coincidents of this qua being and on the contrarieties that belong to it qua being belongs to no other science than philosophy."[31] In conclusion, philosophy (metaphysics) occupies itself with many different things, but not inasmuch as they are diverse or specific, but inasmuch as they are things that are. And what is diverse is eliminated by abstraction, similarly as to how mathematics operates.

And this now allows for the desired solution to the problem posed. "But since everything is said to be with reference to something that is one and common, although so said in many ways, and contraries are in the same position (since they are referred to the primary contrarieties and differentiae of being), and since things of this sort can fall under one science, the puzzle we stated at the start would seem to be resolved—I mean the puzzle as to how there can be one single science of beings that are many and different in genus."[32]

---

[29] Aristotle, *Metaphysics*, XI, 1061a 6-13 (italic ours).

[30] Aristotle, *Metaphysics*, XI, 1061a 29-32.

[31] Aristotle, *Metaphysics*, XI, 1061b 11-17.

[32] Aristotle, *Metaphysics*, XI, 1061b 11-17.

2.4 Essence and Act of Being

Up to here, Aristotle. Over this structure, Thomas Aquinas adds a new and decisive dimension to configure the definitive structure of the metaphysics of being: the composition of the *ens* in essence and act of being.

Thomas Aquinas' essential philosophical project consisted in Christianizing Aristotle. And to that end it was necessary to adapt his metaphysics, since its basic structuring moved along the horizon of the cosmos, it was *immanent*. It seems that Aristotle, like a good Greek, never posed in a radical way the question as to why the ens exists. And, for this reason, his metaphysics of substance does not offer a response to this problem. Substance is simply there. Or, in other words, the ens, "that which is," has been radically explained once one indicates that it is composed of substance and accidents. There is nothing beyond this that needs to be justified. Or, better, the explanation of movement remains pending, an explanation that Aristotle will offer through his particular proposal of the unmoved Mover who moves without being moved, thus being able to cut off the infinite chain of causes.

It seems reasonable to think that in the Aristotelian pure Act one may find *indications* or reference points of the Thomistic vision of being (which drinks more directly from Avicenna). But, even if that were true, it would not eliminate the essential fact: Thomistic metaphysics incorporates, in general terms, a level of radicalization not present in Aristotle or the Greek world, since that level is only reached through the Judeo-Christian concept of creation. The world was not; and, at one given moment, it was. "That which is," was not always and, for the same reason, it could cease to be; that is, the ens is *radically contingent*. And it is contingent in a way that goes far beyond the composition of substance and accidents because, beyond substantial change, it is possible for the ens not to be at all.

Thomas Aquinas theorized that possibility from the starting point of the composition of the *ens* in act of being and essence. The Greeks had already spoken of essence, or of substance. And they brilliantly thematized the possibility that things could be this or that. But Aquinas adds an ulterior depth: the fact, as quotidian as it is incredible, that things *are*. Beyond or above being *this or that*, things, first of all, are, they are there. Because it would be possible for them not to be, not to exist; but they exist, they are. And Thomas Aquinas reflects this radical idea through his concept of *esse* or act of being. "But in any being there are two aspects to be considered, the formal character of its species and the act of being by which it subsists in that species."[33] Or, in another formulation, "ens is said as having being."[34]

Moreover, being, in Thomas Aquinas, does not simply point to the mere datum of existence, like some kind of pure, superficial fact, but rather to the mysterious and tremendous reality which is enclosed within the fact that things are there, present, forming part of reality, the fact that they are.[35] In other words, *the Thomistic* esse *is not a mere add-on to essence*, it is not limited to giving permission to exist to a concept which could have a type of logical existence in the divine mind and upon which existence in fact comes, adding very little to its previous richness.[36] Instead, the opposite occurs: it is the essence which limits the overflowing richness of the act of being, conditioning it to be a concrete ens, the one that possesses *that* essence. In other words, the primacy belongs to being or *esse* (which is act), not to essence. In this way, Thomas escapes any logicism or essentialism. We do not live in a world of logical essences which came to exist, but in a world of entes which are, each one of them, in an individual and unique way, concrete things. And precisely in the fact of being is where their strength and greatness are rooted. Being or *esse* is what is first and definitive, although every ens is always something concrete and limited, except God, whose essence consists only in Being. He is pure Being without any limitation: *Ipsum esse subsistens*.

With this new metaphysical structure, Thomas Aquinas takes a radical step in the interpretation of reality, making possible, at the same time, its connection with Christianity. The Aristotelian substance exists on its own, but this is not so with Thomistic *entes*. They have not given being to themselves, and thus they exist in radical contingence.[37] All being is given, received. And it can only

---

[33] "In quolibet ente est duo considerare, scilicet ipsam rationem speciei, et esse ipsum quo aliquid subsistit in specie illa." Thomas Aquinas, *Quaestiones Disputatae de Veritate*, q. 21, a.1.

[34] "Ens dicitur quasi esse habens." Thomas Aquinas, *In XII libros Metaphysicorum expositio*, XII, Metaph, lect 1., n. 2419.

[35] It is a recognized merit of Gilson and also of Fabro to have brought to light this central fact of Thomistic metaphysics (see, for example, Etienne Gilson, *El ser y los filósofos*, 147-201 and Cornelio Fabro, *Participación y causalidad según Tomás de Aquino*, especially the Introduction and Chapters 1-3). Likewise, among others, Eudaldo Forment, *Ser y persona*, 2nd ed. (Barcelona: Ediciones de la Universidad de Barcelona, 1983), 45-54.

[36] Cf. Suárez, *Disputaciones metafísicas*, Disp. XXXI: "The essence of the finite ens as regards its existence and the distinction between one and the other" (Madrid: Tecnos, 2011).

[37] "For a Greek, being would be, in the end, 'true being,' that is, 'being always,' being that is more or less incorruptible in one measure or the other, at least during a certain period of time, even if segmentary and fragmentary. For the Greeks, the world begins by being

proceed from whom possesses the *esse* by essence, God, who transmits it in the moment of creation. Before creation, only nothingness existed or, more precisely, nothing existed. Thus, creation is *ex nihilo* or, said more precisely, it proceeds from God, from the Being by essence who has created a multiform world in which a gradation of perfection and dignity is observed. And what better way to explain this gradation than through Platonic participation and analogy. Thomas performs here his well-known *synthesis* of Aristotelianism and Platonism in order to close his particular and definitive vision of the cosmos. Each one of the created beings participates in a limited way, according to the possibilities of its essence, in the Infinite Perfection of the Supreme Being. But they all possess being, that is, they are, which makes them all creatures dependent on the Creator in whom that being is sustained and from whom it proceeds. In this way, it is possible to explain the entire creation, from inanimate beings, passing through animals, the human being, and the angels, up to God, in a growing gradation of perfection and beauty.

This is the imposing worldview of Thomas Aquinas, which, from the starting point of Aristotelian metaphysics, through the innovation of the act of being, accounts for the plurality of the cosmos, radicalizes the Greek presuppositions, and shows itself to be compatible with Christianity, in particular with its concept of creation. This gigantic system, which united Aristotle with Christianity through the act of being, is the metaphysics of being.[38]

2.5 Structural Features of the Metaphysics of Being

Having arrived at this point, it is time to summarize the essential features of the metaphysics of being according to the description we have just made:

---

something, whose vicissitudes and internal structure man tries to study. Now, by contrast, the first thing that one thinks about things – and rightly so – is that they could have not been, that is, they may not have been anything but nothing." Zubiri, *Los problemas fundamentales de la metafísica occidental*, 76-77.

[38] In the Heideggerian indictment of the neglect of being, it is striking that the references to Thomas Aquinas are minimal, because it is evident that Thomas grants great value to the *esse* as such. The matter is disputed, and the most benevolent interpretation is that Heidegger had taken up the Suarezian interpretation of the ens: essence + existence. The less benevolent one points in another direction since, taking into account his formation as a Catholic seminarian, it would have been easy for him to know the Thomistic position and to be able to distinguish it from that of Suárez. On this topic, see John D. Caputo, *Heidegger and Aquinas: An Essay on Overcoming Metaphysics* (New York: Fordham University Press, 2003) and Gonzalo Llach, "Heidegger y su interpretación del esse tomista", *Aporía*, 6 (2013), 47-58.

1) Metaphysics of being possesses *thematic universality,* since the object of its study is the whole of reality, that is, of *everything that exists.* Nothing remains outside the glance of metaphysics.

2) It is studied from *the most radical perspective possible: that of being.*

Metaphysics studies everything that exists, but it is not a tautology, that is, it does not have the pretension of knowing everything about everything, but rather, it studies what exists *only* from one perspective: that of existing or that of being. In other words, *while its material object is universal, its formal object is not.* It is, however, the most *radical* object possible, as Alessi indicates: "To apprehend the existent in its formality as existent means, in effect, to reach the final foundation of all reality. Because, in truth, there is nothing previous to being."[39]

3) Structural Universality

The analysis of the ens *qua* ens unveils an overall structure of all of reality through the composition essence/act of being, the transcendental and trans-categorial notions, and the categories. Very different realities exist, but *all of them must necessarily pass through one or another articulation of these notions.* And, to the extent that these realities remit to the essence and not to the act of being, that is, to the extent that it is a question of concrete entes, they must be framed in one or another of the categories.

4) Unifying Character

This fact proportions the metaphysics of being with a "*unifying*" character in line with its universality. "To discover the final foundation of reality means to unveil all that is common to all things, what makes them similar and proximate to each other, conferring to all of them *an air of family* which transcends any differentiation."[40] This relative unification is what permits one, in a certain way, to explain and understand the *gradation of perfection* of the complex world of what is real, from that which is most paltry and poor up to Being by Essence.

---

[39] Adriano Alessi, *Sui sentieri dell'essere. Introduzione alla metafisica,* 2nd ed. (Rome: LAS, 2004), 45. In Alessi, there is a certain change in the traditional terminology, in an existential line, which goes from the ens to the existent, a term which, evidently, does not appear in Thomas Aquinas. On the other hand, Alessi considers that the formal object of metaphysics is also universal, being as existent. But, in our judgment, to attend something from the perspective of "being" (at least for human knowledge) implies not looking at it from other perspectives: what they are in the concrete. In reality, a completely universal science is not possible: the scientific perspective is always sectorial.

[40] Alessi, *Sui sentieri dell'essere. Introduzione alla metafisica,* 46.

5) Radical Primacy of Metaphysics

And, last but not least, since metaphysics proportions the final (or first) structures of all of reality, all the other sciences (philosophical and non-philosophical) *depend on it, since it proportions the first foundations of the ens,* with which all of them occupy themselves. All the sciences, therefore, (and particularly the philosophical ones) *should pass through metaphysics,* since metaphysics supplies them with the basic principles of reality, which are the starting point from which the sciences may construct their particular vision. *Metaphysics, in conclusion, is first philosophy and the rest of the branches of philosophy are second philosophy.* But not only in the sense that they deal with sectorial questions, but also in the sense that they depend on metaphysics in such a radical way that *they cannot even question the principles which metaphysics offers them,* since metaphysics is the most radical science of all and the only one that deals with being. And what is less can never question what is more.

Alessi has expressed it in an unsurpassable way: "Due to the *greater radicality* of its questions, it corresponds to metaphysics to legitimize the first principles which constitute the postulates from which all the sciences proceed. Its *great universality* implies that its conclusions not only have a *universal* value *limited* to the type of realities that are examined, but also an *absolutely universal* value, that is, one that is valid for the 'existent as such' and, therefore, unconditionally referential to any existent."[41] But this is not only Alessi's opinion, but a decisive feature of the metaphysics of being present in any author who accepts it, as Alvira, et al., among others, confirm. "It corresponds to metaphysics, therefore, to exercise an orienting function in the corpus of the sciences, inasmuch as it is the summit of human knowledge of the natural order."[42] And Romera: "Wisdom (metaphysics) is 'hierarchically super-ordered' and it is metaphysics' competence to order, articulate, orient, found, interpret the results of other theoretical and practical sciences."[43]

---

[41] Alessi, *Sui sentieri dell'essere. Introduzione alla metafísica,* 61.

[42] Tomás Alvira, Luis Clavell, Tomás Melendo, *Metafísica* (Pamplona: Eunsa, 1985), 22.

[43] Luis Romera, "L'esigenza della filosofía prima: il suo carattere metafisico e sapienziale," in Luis Romera (ed.), *Ripensare la metafísica* (Rome: Armando, 2005), 125. This does not mean that no authority is granted to the secondary sciences: "The autonomy of the latter is not in contradiction with their relationship with wisdom." (ibid., 127.). But, the scientific (philosophical) primacy corresponds to metaphysics, which imposes a decisive dependence on the rest of the areas of knowledge.

From Universalistic Metaphysics to Personalism as a First Philosophy in Anthropology

Having presented the central theses of the metaphysics of being, it is now the time to begin to reflect on its relationship with personalism and, in particular, with Integral Personalism. What we have to establish is if, and to what extent, personalism depends on this conception of metaphysics; if personalism should be conceptually founded on this conception or not, and to what extent.

We are going to dare to propose our vision of this tangled issue starting with a fundamental division which coincides with the specific contributions attributed to Aristotle and Thomas. It seems to us, in effect, that the categorial question and the question of being, require a very distinct treatment. The why behind this fact will be understood better later on, but we can already anticipate that the fundamental reason that justifies a diversity of analysis is that the categorical question implies a typological categorization or classification of reality that is *universal*, while the Thomistic treatment of being does not necessarily imply this, or at least not in the same measure, or in the same way.

Let us begin, then, with the *categorial question*, a name under which we group or describe the universal typological classification made by Aristotle and whose center are the categories. We are aware that the Aristotelian typification of reality is very complex and that it goes beyond a mere list of categories. In fact, we have already considered the fact that, in addition, it includes the trans-categorial notions, some essential elements of the transcendentals, perhaps also the post-predicamenta. But since it is not possible - and, in fact, not necessary either - to carry out a detailed analysis of all these notions, we will focus on those that constitute the central typification of reality, that is, on the categories. Furthermore, if our conclusions are valid, their extension to other classifications of the real, although it would require important nuances, could be carried out with some ease, as we will have the occasion to verify.

At the beginning of our analysis, we must emphasize that the *universal character* of the Aristotelian metaphysical proposal necessarily implies that *anthropology must pass through metaphysics*. We have already had the opportunity to consider it: metaphysics is the first philosophy, which means, for Aristotle, that it has the ability to determine the fundamental structures which configure *everything* that is real. Consequently, it is necessary to start from metaphysical concepts, as classical (Thomistic, Aristotelian) anthropology does, and subsequently try to see what are the peculiarities that these concepts adopt in the particular case of the human being (or in other areas). This is how one arrives at the famous definition of Boethius: the person as an individual substance of a rational nature. Since the world is composed of substances – the ens is fundamentally substance – the person cannot fail to be a substance; although certainly a very peculiar one.

In view of these reflections, the first thing we must do is determine the validity of this perspective: *do the Aristotelian categories provide a good substrate for anthropology?* This is the first end we should attempt to tie (or untie).

3.1 The Anthropological Deficiencies of the Aristotelian Categories

Our first thesis is that the Aristotelian categories present *serious deficiencies* for constructing an adequate anthropology. We will attempt to justify our position by posing the problem both in general and through concrete cases. And the first thing that we want to signal is that it is a structural difficulty that proceeds from the very configuration of the Aristotelian proposal. Since the categories have to be strictly universal, they can only do so by being extraordinarily abstract (and general), the only way in which they can encompass all of reality. It happens, however, that the human being is very specific and peculiar, and traveling the path that goes from the most universal and general to something so specific and peculiar becomes so difficult that, in practice, this path is never traveled completely, which generates at least two fundamental problems.[1]

a) The Darkening of What Is Specifically Human

Starting from the generality, from what "all things are," that is, from the categories, carries with it the grave danger of never coming to truly and profoundly know "what *only* man is." Why? Because the path that goes from "what is general" to the human being is too long and tortuous and there are many chances to get lost or to stray, and, above all, to never reach the end, remaining in what *is common* and not entering into what is specifically human: that by which man is man.

Let us illustrate the matter with some examples, although later we will head with one of them, action, with special depth. The human person is characterized by having a lived experience of himself through a consciousness in which he

---

[1] These problems are discussed in detail in Juan Manuel Burgos, *La experiencia integral. Un método para el personalismo* (Madrid: Palabra, 2015), 252ff.

not only knows himself, but in which he inhabits generating the space necessary for the existence of the self. Now, does this reality occur in any other of the beings on our planet? The answer must be negative. We can find partly similar structures perhaps in the superior animals, although we are not going to go beyond the level of conjecture in our analysis, since it is highly improbable that we may come to really know the experience that they have of themselves. But what is clear, in any case, is that in the human being that structure exists. Moreover, it defines his essence to the point that we cannot conceive of him without it.[2]

Now, can we gain access to this phenomenon by following the procedure of the *metaphysical cascade* that goes from the general to the particular? It seems very complicated and, in fact, the tradition that is based on the metaphysics of being has not succeeded in doing so. Why? Because the *ens (as a concept) whose contents are described through the categories does not have subjectivity.* The Aristotelian categories do not include the notion of subjectivity *and they cannot include it* because this aspect of reality is sectorial, limited to humans and perhaps - to a certain extent - to superior animals. For this reason, the ens, in its generality, cannot be subjective because, since it can only include what is common to everything that exists, it has no choice but to constitute itself *by reduction* and, more concretely, by disregarding what is specifically human since, precisely because it is specific, it *only* takes place in man.

Faced with this reasoning, one could object that in the concept or notion of ens everything that exists is implicitly included, because everything that exists is some type of ens. This, to some degree, is true; but it does not go beyond being a merely formal and empty affirmation which, for that reason, has no consequences. In the ens, in some sense, everything is included. But the only thing that is thus affirmed is that everything that exists, exists, which is tautological. And if we are not conscious of *what* actually exists, that existence becomes virtual and irrelevant, it becomes a non-existence on which it is impossible to reflect.

b) The Possible Deformation of What Is Specifically Human

Something similar happens with affectivity. The ens, in the reality of its constitution through the categories, does not have feelings and cannot have them because not all beings feel. Therefore, it cannot be surprising that feelings have a secondary place in the metaphysics of being. And, when they do appear,

---

[2] Cf. Karol Wojtyła, *La subjetividad y lo irreductible en el hombre*, in Karol Wojtyła, *El hombre y su destino* (Madrid: Palabra, 2005), 25-39. See G. Holub, *Understanding the Person. Essays on the Personalism of Karol Wojtyła* (Berlin-New York: Peter Lang, 2021).

a poor explanation of them is offered, an explanation derived from the metaphysical cascade, which usually consists in *an application of the concept of animal sensitivity to the human world*. But this approach is not only poor but *false* because the human being is *not* an animal. As von Hildebrand indicates, "it would be completely erroneous to think that the bodily sensations of men are the same as those of animals since the bodily pain, the pleasure and the instincts that a person experiences have a radically different character from those of an animal. The bodily feelings and the impulses in man are certainly not spiritual experiences, but they are, without a doubt, personal experiences."[3]

Here we come across the second anthropological problem derived from the use of the Aristotelian categories: the possible *deformation* of what is specifically human. Polo has affirmed that from the perspective of traditional metaphysics, one arrives at a "correct anthropology, but one that falls short: it does not err, it is not mistaken, but its thematic development is scarce."[4] This is doubtless a true statement. But what happens when an anthropology falls short? When it does not adequately present the *essential* aspects of the human person? What happens is that this anthropology – despite not being erroneous – *presents, in practice, a deformed vision of the human being* by hiding or not being able to notice some of its *principal* characteristic features. And this is what happens, in our judgment, with the anthropologies that take the Aristotelian categories as their exclusive presupposition, because from these categories we cannot extract affectivity, subjectivity, interpersonal relations, personal narrativity, etc. For this reason, there are many possibilities for an anthropology that is "constructed" from the starting point of the categories to be not only limited or poor, but deformed, to the extent to which it proposes a vision of the person in which essential elements are lacking.

c) From the Act to Action: An Analysis of a Trans-Categorical Notion

To go deeper into these affirmations, we are going to study in detail a specific case, that of action, taking advantage of a work by S. Brock in which the metaphysical cascade procedure is perfectly and consciously explicit.[5] Action (the act) is not, according to our classification, properly speaking a category, but a trans-categorical notion. But this does not affect the consequences of this

---

[3] Dietrich von Hildebrand, *El corazón* (Madrid: Palabra, 2002), 62. English: *The Heart* (South Bend, IN: St. Augustine's Press, 2007).

[4] Leonardo Polo, *Antropología trascendental. I. La persona humana* (Pamplona: Eunsa, 1999), 31.

[5] Cf. Stephen L. Brock, *Acción y conducta. Tomás de Aquino y la teoría de la acción* (Barcelona: Herder, 2002). English: *Action and Conduct. Thomas Aquinas and the Theory of Action* (Bloomsbury: T& T Clark 1997).

analysis, since what we want to check is the validity or invalidity of the metaphysical cascade, of the analytical path that goes from the general to the particular, as well as the convenience or not of using universal concepts for anthropology.

The first thing Brock points out when analyzing the concept of action in Thomas Aquinas is that the latter starts with *action in general*, to the point that he "uses the term 'action' somewhat equivocally. 'Action' corresponds to the Latin *actio*, and in Thomistic use, to the infinitive *agere*, taken as a noun. He often openly applies those terms, and the finite forms of *agere*, to what is done by non-human and non-personal subjects. One of his favorite examples of action is the fire heating something up. However, on other occasions, he makes an explicit call to restrict the term to the human or voluntary. For example, when he comments on Book II of Aristotle's *Physics*, he stresses that action belongs properly to him who is master of his acts: *eius autem proprie est agere, quod habet dominium sui actus*. The expression 'owner of one's own acts' is one of the ways of describing agents who have free choice, i.e., agents capable of voluntary or human acts. This same doctrine is repeated several times in the *Summa Theologiae*. Yet, surprisingly, both the *Commentary on the Physics* and the *Summa Theologiae* also contain extensive treatments of the 'action' of physical, non-voluntary subjects. Some of them are very close to the passages in which the term is appropriated for human acts."[6]

How then is one to proceed in order to determine the specific meaning of the notion of action? Brock solves the problem by coining the term "analogous equivocal" that ends up being identified with the classic concept of analogy. The "analogous equivocals" can be studied seriously because although they refer to a set of diverse and even heterogeneous meanings, it is possible to determine a *primary nucleus* that unites the meanings and gives them unity. Logically, such a nucleus cannot be perfectly defined, since it would then "expel" the rest of the meanings, but it can achieve enough precision to avoid the risk of error. This is what happens with the term *actus*. By using it, we know in general terms what we are talking about, although that generic meaning must be specified in each case, which can be expressed, according to Brock, saying that "the 'common notion' of *actus* would be '_____ operation.' Remove the blank and you have the primary sense, *actus simpliciter*. Each secondary sense will require filling in the blank and doing it in such a way that the reference of the term to the operation is qualified."[7] In short, *actus* refers in

---

[6] Brock, *Acción y conducta*, 20.

[7] Brock, *Acción y conducta*, 23. This description can be compared with Wojtyła's position: "We call action exclusively the *conscious activity* of man. No other activity merits that

a generic way to the concept of operation, but the concrete ways in which it manifests itself can be quite varied, from the idea of movement to the culmination of that movement as form or perfection.

This way of proceeding makes some sense; but we have already warned, and we will come back to it later, that this way of proceeding is established through a leveling of minimums. Since the general concept of act must cover everything that is real, it must have the *least* possible content. Brock, of course, is fully aware of the originality of what is human; but he uses this procedure on purpose because he wants to study what is *common*, the substrate that makes possible or is present *in any type of dynamism*, as well as to avoid an abrupt separation between human beings and other realities. For this reason, he has no difficulty in concluding that "a rigorous understanding of freedom does not even seem an essential element of the general concept of action."[8] Since not all actions or acts are free – more still, since the majority of them are not – studying action in a general way implies dispensing with freedom, since otherwise the investigation would be falsified by privileging one very relevant but specific case.

In summary, Brock seeks to understand "human action through the consideration of the characteristics common to being a human action and to being a physical action,"[9] which leads him to a basic model of action (*actus* or operation) very close to the physical movement of an Aristotelian type described in these terms by St. Thomas: "the first thing by virtue of which it can be conjectured that one thing proceeds from another is by movement, since from the moment in which by a movement the disposition of a being changes, there is no doubt that this happens due to some cause. Hence, action, in its primitive meaning, signified the origin of movement; and for this reason, just as movement, insofar as it is received in the mobile by virtue of the agent, is called *passion*, so also the origin of movement, as soon as it begins in the agent and ends in what is moved, is called *action*".[10]

The results obtained by Brock using this methodology are as follows. The common features that characterize action are: "effectiveness," "a certain type of causality," "finality" and the "agent-patient relationship," to which one must

---

name. [...] When we say action, there is no need to add 'human' to it because only human activity is action." Wojtyła, *Persona y acción* (Madrid: Palabra, 2017), 61; English: *Person and act.*

[8] Brock, *Acción y conducta*, 58-59.

[9] Brock, *Acción y conducta*, 29.

[10] Thomas Aquinas, *Summa Theologiae*, I, q. 41, a. 1, ad 2.

add that the will appears as a tendency that "moves and is moved."[11] What may one comment on these conclusions? Undoubtedly, this set of notions has speculative relevance and points out decisive elements of "the" action, but, in relation to our topic, one must inevitably note that they are weighed down by a fundamental factory defect: *they are not anthropological concepts* and, therefore, they are unable to adequately show the reality of *personal dynamisms*.

Take, for example, *finality*. The Aristotelian teleology that supports this conception involves the affirmation that all beings tend towards ends proposed by their nature. This is, therefore, the starting point, the fundamental notion from which one must also construct *human* finality. And what does the Thomistic theory of human action propose? It indicates that man too tends towards the ends that his nature proposes, but *freely*; that is, he can reject his ends or freely accept them. And, in the latter case, he can choose the means that lead him towards those ends. This description undoubtedly reflects part of what takes place in human action. But does it reflect it properly? Does it describe *the essentials of human action correctly*? It seems that this is not the case because there is much, too much, that remains unsaid.[12]

First of all, we must keep in mind that a *structure based on tendencies* cannot explain *human* dynamicity properly since it does not leave sufficient space for freedom. It gives the impression that man is remote-controlled from his birth towards a series of pre-established ends, and his freedom consists solely in the possibility of accepting or rejecting those ends as well as choosing the means that will lead him to the realization of the chosen option. But this is not true. Man *can also choose his own ends*, at least to some extent. Our path is not completely pre-established from the beginning. It is we, in part, who decide what and who we want to be. It can even be affirmed that man's creativity generates new ends, for example, through technology that invents new worlds that did not exist before and that brings with them their sources of finality. Furthermore, one must consider that human action is not, strictly speaking, a tendency, but rather a free *response* generated by the subject faced with values. In other words, although there are tendencies in man, *what is specifically human is not to tend towards something, but to respond*; to activate a free response. Which also implies a *revision of the concept of causality*. The causality of free human action, in fact, is different from the Aristotelian causality structure derived from the analysis of movement, since freedom moves without

---

[11] Brock, *Acción y conducta*, 60 and ff.

[12] A detailed analysis of the concept of human nature from this perspective can be found in Juan Manuel Burgos, *Repensar la naturaleza humana* (Mexico: Siglo XXI, 2018).

being moved, it is an absolute principle, *causa sui*, which is situated on the level of what is strictly personal.[13]

It must also be kept in mind that man does not seek external ends without at the same time seeking himself because he is an end for himself. For this reason, human teleology is only correct if it is completed with a self-teleology which Wojtyła explains in this way: "It is necessary to observe that the term 'self-determination' indicates, at the same time, both the fact that only the subject or the personal self is determined (and acts), and the fact that such a personal self as a subject determines itself. Consequently, in this dynamic relationship, the self is placed as an object in front of itself, an object of the will understood as the faculty that determines the subject. Precisely in this relationship is contained *in some sense the 'nucleus' of man's self-teleology*."[14] This allows us to conclude that the finalistic structure in man must be subsumed under the concept of a freedom that consists in the subject's capacity for self-determination, which in turn allows one to affirm that "the will appears above all as a *property of the person*, and only secondarily as a faculty."[15]

Enough has now been said, because our objective is not to make a theory of freedom but to *compare the explanation derived from universal principles with an analysis based directly and exclusively on the experience of human action.* And the result jumps out. The vision of freedom that derives from the finalist conception of action designed by Aristotle and Thomas (and taken up by Brock) falls far short of showing and explaining what is proper to free human action, which does not reside in finalistic tendentiality but precisely in what remains outside of it.[16]

And it falls short – this is the point that we wanted to show – because *the concepts from which it begins are not adequate for the objective intended to be achieved.* Human action is free. And freedom *only occurs in man.* Therefore, it is never going to be possible to carry out an adequate analysis of freedom if we

---

[13] The need to revise causality to adapt it to personal being has already been intuited starting with Kant and noted with special clarity within personalism. See Borden P. Bowne, *Personalism* (Cambridge: The Riverside Press, 1908): Ch. IV: *Mechanical or volitional causality*, and Xavier Zubiri, *Inteligencia y razón* (Madrid, Alianza Editorial, 2008), 238.

[14] Karol Wojtyła, *Transcendencia de la persona en el obrar y autoteleología del hombre*, in *El hombre y su destino*, 142-143. English: Karol Wojtyła, "The Transcendence of the Person in Action and Man's Self-Teleology," in A.T. Tymieniecka (ed.), *The Teleologies in Husserlian Phenomenology. Analecta Husserliana* (1979).

[15] Wojtyła, *Persona y acción*, 170 (italics ours).

[16] A similar analysis could be performed on the ability of the concept of substance to show or, at least, assume human subjectivity; the adequacy of the notion of nature to reflect the free dynamism of man, etc.

start from non-human universal categories and later on apply them to human beings. We will always fall short, mediated by concepts that will weigh down our analysis. One might think that these limits could be resolved by incorporating these topics from the outside, from another type of analysis, such as anthropology. This type of complement would doubtless improve our vision of the person, and we consider that it, in fact, is being performed by part of current Thomism. But what we are trying to highlight is that: 1) These contributions have to be integrated *from outside* into the fundamental scheme provided by the categories. Therefore, they will never be able to be thought of as elements that structure the person, but as qualifications of the categorial concepts. In other words, their influence on the construction of anthropology will always be limited. 2) By having to integrate these contributions into a different and impersonal previous structure, it is very possible that they lose part of their wealth and originality. 3) Finally, it may happen that these contributions will not even be grasped in all their vigor and strength since if the basic structure of reality is categorial (Aristotelian) everything will be looked at under that prism, and what remains outside of it will not even be detected or only in a very weak way.

3.2 Personalist Categories

The previous analyses have shown the anthropological limits of the categories of the metaphysics of being and their use through the method of the metaphysical cascade. The beginning of the cascade is situated in the notion-concept of ens and, from there, it tries to reach anthropology. But this procedure - as we have observed - has two main problems.

1. The first is that the notion of ens on which it is based is, in fact, *very formal*; an abstract, universal, and generic reality about which one could doubt if it really exists. This observation is often answered by saying that the meaning of the ens in Aristotle or in Thomas is not this. It is not a general notion, but rather it refers to the existing and concrete entes; therefore, it would have all the wealth of reality. This, in part, is true, but perhaps not entirely. Undoubtedly, in Thomas Aquinas and Aristotle, there is a realist impulse that leads them to study things that exist, that are given, that are there presenting themselves to human intelligence. In a word, *the things that are, that is to say, the entes*. This is the primary nucleus of any realist position: to analyze what is given, as it is given, without thinking for a moment that it is a product of the human mind or is given only on an intentional level.

So far, our agreement is complete. Now it happens that Thomas (and Aristotle) does not stop here. He goes one step further that leads him to determine the *characteristics of every ens*. And this is when things (perhaps) start to go wrong. Because from this analysis emerges a specific concept of ens, very complex and structured, which includes the essence/act of being composition, the transcendentals, etc., and which *must be present in any subsequent step of thought* since everything that exists is, necessarily, an ens. We are, precisely, at the beginning of the cascade, where the water begins to fall and where a logical-constructive process begins which, frequently, does not start from the real thing but from the *notion* of ens. "The first thing that the understanding conceives, as what is best known, and in which it solves all its other concepts, is the ens... Therefore, it is necessary that all other concepts of the understanding be taken as *additions* to the ens."[17]

There is, of course, a non-logicistical interpretation of this expression, which remits to the purest and more experiential realism. Thomas, with this type of expressions, would simply be affirming that things are there, that they are. And, of course, he is indeed affirming this. But staying there would mean ignoring the undoubtable logicistic vein that nestles in his mind. Thomas Aquinas, following Aristotle's metaphysical project, intends to offer an overall, structured vision of reality. And that vision is founded on the universal characteristics derived from the analysis of the ens. Doubtless, Thomas Aquinas is not a rationalist, so his intention will never be that *everything* come out of this analysis without new references to the real, but there is a tension in his analysis that shows a dual path or, in other words, a certain lack of coherence which brings with it the result that the concrete existent remains subsumed, at least on occasion, by the logical apparatus. It is a tension which is perfectly reflected in this text by González Alvarez: "The conceptual development of the ens does not occur as if the multiplicity of ideas arose from the idea of ens. The ens as ens is neither a spout nor a source. Like the idea of ens, all other ideas have their origin in abstraction and in experience. What does happen is that all other ideas are determinations of the ens, from which the entire concatenation of concepts proceeds as from its center. In *De Veritate*, q. 1, a. 1, St. Thomas offers us an outline of this concatenation of the concepts closest to the ens. That which the understanding conceives as what is best known and in which the understanding resolves all the other concepts is the ens. From this it follows that all other concepts must be formed by additions to the concept of ens."[18] And, in the same sense, "there is no science *of the ens*, but there can be a science *of all the entes*. If we disregard all their differences and consider that in which they are

---

[17] Thomas Aquinas, *De veritate*, q. 1, a. 1, resp. (italics ours). This is the line of thinking which, in some way, leads to rationalist ontology. "Quoniam ontologia de ente in genere agit, ea demostrare debet quae entibus omnibus sive absolute, sive sub data quaedam conditione convenient." Wolff, *Philosophia prima sive ontologia methodo scientifica pertractata*, paragraph 8, page 3.

[18] González Álvarez, *Tratado de Metafísica*, 114.

fundamentally similar to each other, the pure formality of the fact that they are, we will do first philosophy, the science of all entes insofar as they are entes, or more briefly, science of the ens qua ens." [19] Without wishing to disdain or underestimate in any way the realistic streak of Thomism, it seems difficult not to accept that this type of expressions brings to light a formalist background that, moreover, would allow one to explain the strong influence of rationalism on the first wave of neo-Thomism.

2. The second problem we find is that the path that leads from this formal ens to reality is too long and tortuous to be traveled satisfactorily. In fact, it is not going to be possible to reach the personal existence with the desired fullness. From the Aristotelian categories to the personal realm there is such a long journey that when the destination is reached, one does not have the strength to apprehend the object in its rich originality. We have verified this for human action: if the analysis begins with local movement, one must journey so far to reach the structure of self-determination that, in fact, no one has made the journey.

3. Behind or in connection with these difficulties, there is another problem, which I have on occasion referred to as the *Greek ballast*.[20] The Greek world did not know the concept of person and had, in Wojtyła's terminology, a *cosmological* understanding of the human being. Man was a very special thing but, in the end, one more thing in the world, a being among the rest of the beings. So, for the Greeks, there was no reason why applying universal categories to man *as well* would be problematic. And this is what we find in Aristotle. Every being has a nature responsible for its dynamism. Therefore, man must also have a nature, but with special features such as rationality or the will that allow him not only to know his tendencies but to follow or reject them. This explanation, in our judgment, is as true as it is limited because, in this way, the human being barely manages to emerge from the cosmological world and show his peculiar originality, namely, that he can not only freely perform some actions, but that he is *structurally* free. In other words, the notion of "nature" designed for the non-free world can only be used in the context of the human being with great limits, something that modernity has clearly noted.[21]

---

[19] González Álvarez, *Tratado de Metafísica*, 114.

[20] Burgos, *La experiencia integral*, 281-289.

[21] Modernity noticed the internal rigidity of the concept of nature and either rejected it or limited it to the biological realm. This being true, one must conserve from the ancient concept of nature its valid dimension: the essential community of all persons, their radical equality. A term that may reflect this fact without falling into the limits of

The same thing happens with the concept of substance, as Julián Marías has noted. "When, already in scholasticism, an attempt has been made to think about the person philosophically, the notions that have been decisive are not those coming from these contexts, but those of 'property' or 'subsistence' (*hypóstasis*). Boethius' famous definition, so influential - *persona est rationalis naturae individua substantia* - has started from the Aristotelian notion of *ousía* or *substantia*, thought up in the first place for 'things,' always explained with the eternal examples of the statue and the bed, founded on the old Greek ideal of the 'independent' or sufficient, of the 'separable' (*khoriston*). That this substance or thing that we call 'person' is rational, will undoubtedly be important, but not enough to rework over this character of the *ousía* and modify its way of being, its way of reality. The person is a *hypostasis* or *suppositum* like the others, only that the person is of a rational nature."[22] We can, therefore, use the notion of substance to explain the human being, and so has it been done for centuries, but it is a problematic concept because in man there are personal structures that only with much difficulty can be reflected through this notion (which was conceived for things). Consider, for example, the idea of personal self or identity, associated in turn with the notions of interiority and subjectivity. Is it possible to reflect these characteristics through the Aristotelian concept of substance? It seems difficult to offer an affirmative answer.

How can we resolve all these difficulties? The adequate way, in our judgment, is to think of the human person from *personalistic categories*, that is, from *categories elaborated exclusively for the human being, who is a person*, the meaning of category being here similar to the Aristotelian meaning, that is, a *mode of being*. The difference with Aristotle is that we understand that these categories can only have a sectorial value, restricted to one sphere of reality. In this sense, *the personalist categories reflect the proper and specific modes of being of the person and only of the person*. Therefore, every person, by the simple fact of being a person, will be structured and configured by these

---

Aristotelian teleology is that of "humanity." "Personalism places among its key ideas the affirmation of the unity of humanity in space and in time, intuited by some schools from the end of Antiquity and affirmed in the Judeo-Christian tradition." Emmanuel Mounier, *El personalismo* (Madrid: ACC, 1998), 26; English: *Personalism* (London: Routledge and Kegan Paul, 1952).

[22] Julián Marías, *Antropología metafísica* (Madrid: Alianza, 1987), 41; English: *Metaphysical Anthropology: The Empirical Structure of Human Life* (University Park, Pa.: Pennsylvania State University Press, 1971).

categories. And *only* person will be so, because no other being has the structure of personal being.[23]

It does not seem to us that there is any other way to adequately grasp and reflect what is peculiar and proper to personal being. The abyssal and essential difference that runs between human beings and the rest of reality prevents a different procedure from being used. Any progressive analytical system that goes from less to more will not work, because more can never come out of less. The issue, therefore, is to recognize the diversity of reality and to be consistent with it. The diverse must be treated diversely; it must be faced in its specificity without depending on categories that distort that understanding of reality, working, in practice, in a Kantian way; that is, forcing reality to adapt to the formal structure defined by those categories. If, on the contrary, *we analyze the personal facts of experience directly,* "I want something," or "I feel," or "I love," we will not be mediated by categories, formalizations or pre-understandings from other sectors of reality. We will confront, directly and without mediations, radical human phenomena: identity, subjectivity, interpersonality. We will be respectful with what is real, that is, we will be realists. And, to the extent of our possibilities and of the tradition which we inhabit, we will be in a position to design concepts much more appropriate to the human person.

From all that has been said, it should not be concluded that we do not ascribe any value to the Aristotelian categorization of the real. It is evident that it reflects essential aspects of the world that cannot be ignored in any self-respecting philosophy. And much less if it has the pretension of being realist. What we sustain is that, because of their structural universality, they cannot be

---

[23] The Heidegger of *Being and Time* notes a similar necessity, although he uses the term existential where we employ the term personalist categories: "All the explanations which arise from the analytics of the *Dasein* are reached by looking toward its structure of existence. And since these characters of being of the *Dasein* are determined from existentiality, we call them *existentials*. One should rigorously distinguish them from the determinations of the being of the ens which does not have the form of being of the *Dasein*, determinations to which we give the name of *categories*. [...] Existentials and categories are the two fundamental possibilities of the characters of being. The respective ens must be interrogated in a different way each time: as a *who* (existence) or as a *what* (a being there, in the widest sense)." Martin Heidegger, *Ser y tiempo* (Madrid: Trotta, 2013), 65-66; English: *Being and Time* (Harper Collins, 2008). But the development of this difference walks a different terrain than ours because, in his judgment, "what blocks or launches on a false path the fundamental question about the being of the *Dasein* is the habitual orientation toward Ancient-Christian anthropology, whose insufficient ontological foundations go unnoticed even to personalism and the philosophy of life." Heidegger, *Ser y tiempo*, 70.

used as such categories by anthropology, although the contents that the Aristotelian categories intend to reflect should be taken into account by anthropology. Take the concept of substance, for example. The irrenounceable contribution that Aristotle managed to transmit thanks to the concept of substance is the articulated stability of reality (against Heraclitus and Parmenides). Not everything is flow or movement, nor is it pure stability. There are things capable of remaining in themselves, maintaining their essential being through changes. And there are others that do not possess that quality. This is the thesis that should be maintained, particularly for the person, if we do not want to transform the person into a stream of consciousness as Hume did. But, *how do we do it?* This is the question.

Personally, I consider that it is not possible to do it through the concept of substance as it was elaborated by Aristotle, for at least two reasons. The first one, already pointed out, is that it does not seem possible to introduce subjectivity into that Aristotelian elaboration. The second is that the concept of substance is inseparable from that of accident and this pair of notions claims the ability to explain *everything* that is real. But *can reality be divided exclusively into substance and accidents?* The answer is simply no. Reality, especially personal reality, is much more complex and we do not understand why it should be reduced *exclusively to two possibilities.* And if our philosophical system forces us to do so, these two parameters will cease to be mirrors of reality and will become Kantian forms that force reality to adapt to them. The correct solution should be to travel another path: to express what is valid in the Aristotelian intuitions, in this case, the necessary permanence of "something" in the midst of the flow of personal activity which can account for the fact that the person continues being the same person even though he or she changes. Now, this "something," which is responsible for maintaining the identity of the person, *cannot be impersonal* as, in fact, the Aristotelian substance is. *What is impersonal cannot account for what is personal.* That is why it is so complicated to associate the concept of substance with that of the subject or the self. Our thesis is that the notion of substance should be replaced by that of a self, conceived of with ontological density, that is, not as a superficial phenomenon of consciousness, but as the last root of the person, ultimately responsible, not only for identity but for ontological stability.[24]

---

[24] We have gone deeper into these ideas in our debate with John F. Crosby. Cf. Juan Manuel Burgos, "El yo como raíz ontológica de la persona. Reflexiones a partir de John F. Crosby", *Quién* 6 (2017), 33-54; John F. Crosby, "On solitude, subjectivity and substantiality.

This is not, however, the moment to present this proposal in detail. We were seeking to show the anthropological deficiencies of the Aristotelian categories and to define our alternative proposal, the personalist categories. And we believe we have done so. This solution, however, leaves in the air a question not explicitly answered. Admitting that the Aristotelian categories do not adequately reflect what is real, should the solution to this difficulty necessarily pass through a sectorial analysis of reality? Or is there a possibility of a more accurate universal analysis? In other words, is it possible to substitute the personalist categories for another, more adequate universal categorial structure, or should we simply abandon the pretension of a universal analysis of reality?

3.3 Do universal categories exist?

The question about the existence or not of universal categories could be divided into two aspects, interconnected but, to a certain extent, different. The first one is that of their existence; the second is that of their possible conceptualization. The status that metaphysics should have in its categorial dimension and in relation to anthropology, which is the aspect that occupies us in this chapter, will be derived, in the end, from the answer we give to these two questions. We are going to attempt to respond to these two questions and then bring the chapter to a close by drawing a conclusion about the relationship between personalism and metaphysics.

a) The Improbable Existence of Universal Categories

We understand this question in the sense, already mentioned, of the categories that reflect universal aspects *of everything that is real*; aspects, modes of being, or whatever we want to call them that are found universally in *all things (or in very wide sectors)*. Personally, it seems complex to me to admit this because reality is so incredibly diverse that finding a least common multiple of what exists becomes an enormous task. What could be found in common between a molecule, a granite rock, a plant, an amoeba, a dinosaur, a prosthesis, a cell phone, an idea, the internet and man? Let us remember that we are not yet situating ourselves on the ontological plane, of being, but on the categorial plane, that is, the one that refers to *specific modes* of being or of reality occurring. Because the first answer to our question could point to analogy, to the fact that all things are, or are real. But now, this answer is not useful. We will return to this question in the next chapter, but for the moment, what we need to try to elucidate is whether all existing realities have common modes of being.

Certainly, we can find some type of unity, or family resemblance[25] between everything that is given: it usually has a certain degree of materiality, it is located in space, it has some type of dynamism. But specifying much more does not seem very feasible, with the serious drawback, moreover, that when these terms are used, it is not evident that one is talking about the same thing, which, in some way, would invalidate the character of universality. For example, are there categories applicable to human corporeality and to the materiality of a rock? Of course, we can turn to the ubiquitous *analogy* and claim that there is something called matter that makes them partly the same and partly different. But, frankly, this is not enough. If we want to be faithful to what exists, we must define it *with precision*. Generalities are not enough. Even though Aristotle said it, we cannot put in the same category a "healthy" apple and a physician, because an apple is a fruit and the physician is a human being. Nor can we put in the same bag the movement of a billiard ball and the self-determination of a personal being that, among other things, is carried out without movement. "Analogy," as Aubenque points out, "homogenizes the unsimilar and dissolves the graduation in commensurability."[26] So, if care is not taken, recourse to this notion may in practice be a pragmatistic option to blur problems for which one does not have an answer, a type of "forward evasion."[27]

There are two solutions to this situation. The more drastic would be to *dispense with categorial metaphysics*. Let us assume point blank that there are no universal structures that encompass everything that exists. It is doubtless a radical option, especially for the realist tradition associated with Aristotle and Thomas. But is it problematic or risky? Could it affect the constitution or the safeguarding of meaning? Not really. In daily life, there is no need to universalize, unify or integrate. A dog is different from a taxi and a movie. They are different things, each one with its qualities. I interact with those that interest me. And that's it. And if I have intellectual concerns, I try to understand more deeply

---

[25] Cf. Alessi, *Sui sentieri dell'essere. Introduzione alla metafisica,* 46

[26] Pierre Aubenque, *¿Hay que deconstruir la metafísica?* (Madrid: Encuentro, 2009), 84.

[27] "With regard to the connotation, I will remember that it is one of the three ideas that are used as a type of key, a *passe-partout,* in Scholastic metaphysics; the other two are analogy and participation; so, there are several concepts and with them the problems are resolved right way. But it cannot be so at all. One must think, in each concrete case, about what that means." Xavier Zubiri, *Sobre la realidad* (Madrid: Alianza Editorial, 2001), 117.

what each of them consists in. It does not seem necessary for them to have anything in common.

Someone might point out that this solution establishes a *discontinuity* in reality. Each thing would exist independently of the others without any common aspect, which would imply that man inhabits an arbitrary and disconnected world in which it would be impossible to establish a Meaning. But, is this necessarily so? From the fact that there are no structurally universal categories, does it follow that we cannot give meaning to reality? That reality would become disjointed and incomprehensible? Frankly, one cannot see why it has to be impossible to find meaning in reality just because we cannot describe it through universal categories. In fact, the majority of humanity does not use these categories, which does not prevent them from giving meaning to reality (with or without the help of a religion) or affirming meaninglessness if they reach this conclusion. Do universal categories contribute much to this solution? It does not look like it, since meaning should be determined from the starting point of what really exists, which is singular.

This path leads to *categorial sectorization*. Since reality is so diverse, we should adapt to it with flexibility and fidelity, study each type of being in its strict and peculiar originality, and see what are the specific categories or structures that configure them and through which they are expressed. In the case of persons, it leads to personalist categories, just as, in the case of animals, it would lead to "animal categories," which it would probably be convenient to subsequently subdivide.

One last note before continuing. *Denying the existence of universal categories in no way implies denying the possibility of stable or absolute truths.* This thesis does not affect Meaning. These are two completely different questions, although they can be mistakenly identified. The existence of stable truths refers to the third meaning of metaphysics, which responds to the need to define stable units of meaning that can be grasped by the intelligence in truth. We do not deny this at all. On the contrary, we affirm it emphatically. The notion of person is a good example. We affirm that the person has strictly peculiar traits such as her freedom, intelligence, and heart, unified by the self, which grant her a unique dignity.[28] These are absolute and stable truths. But they are not universal concepts. Only human beings are persons. Animals are another type of beings, just like plants and television sets. Likewise, we could enumerate many other truths. What is denied in the solution that we propose is something very specific: *that all reality is configured from similar patterns* at the categorical

---

[28] Cf. Burgos, *Personalist Anthropology*.

level. This and only this is what is denied. Therefore, the denial of a possible universal structure of reality does not imply any kind of relativism.

b) Limits in the Conceptualization of the Possible Universal Categories

There is, in any case, a less drastic response. Assuming that the world is tremendously diverse and different, something not very difficult to accept, it can be considered that, in any case, all things (realities, entes, is not the issue at the moment) have to have something in common just for being there: a basic structure, some common features, a unitary character that makes them be this thing and not another, a certain dynamism, etc. Universality could be founded on this. I do not completely reject this possibility, but I consider that the result of this approach is almost inevitably poor because it is necessarily based on two premises: *1) it must be a theory of minimums;* consequently, *2) the concepts used must have a high degree of ambiguity.*

If the metaphysical proposal wants to be universal, it must eliminate any element of specific individual richness. It cannot consider sensitivity, intelligence or life, because all of this refers to concrete beings. It must cut low, at the inferior level, at that which is so common that it is always present. Take, for example, unity. Every being (ens, thing), insofar as it is, is one, because otherwise we would have to speak of a plurality of beings. Similarly, all beings have some dynamicity (Brock) and one can try to analyze what is common to every being inasmuch as it is dynamic. But we already know that the result of this kind of analysis is very limited. And it has as an inevitable collateral effect the fact that it produces very ambiguous notions because a delineated and precise notion is only applicable to specific realities. Let us take up again the example of unity. The notion of one which we elaborate or construct should be applied to rocks, plants, animals, technological products and persons, because they are all one, but in their own way. So, if the notion of unity that is designed is very precise, it will work for some things but not for others. And if, instead of considering one of the transcendentals, whose universality is easier to sustain, we go into the categorial level, thematizing, for example, where and when, then the question becomes still more complicated.[29]

---

[29] Aubenque considers that this objective generates an internal contradiction within the Aristotelian system itself which is summarized "in a fundamental aporia [which] could be formulated according to these three propositions which Aristotle sustains, one after the other, and which, however, are of such a nature that one cannot accept two of them without rejecting the third:

In short, although we have attempted to give a certain validity to universal categorization, the analysis sends us back to the conclusions already reached. It is an impossible attempt because such an elevated level of universalization leads to generality, that is, to vagueness. And vagueness is incompatible with the scientific character as it had been intended by Aristotle himself, who emphasizes that science can only deal with something "determined."[30]

These difficulties, it should be added, *are not proper only to Aristotelian metaphysics*. We find them *in any metaphysics with claims of universality* because it is a structural problem. Zubiri, for example, has been perfectly aware of the difficulties of Aristotelian metaphysics and has attempted to overcome them through a *new metaphysics*. Thus, to avoid the problems we were referring to when dealing with substance, he elaborated the concept of "substantivity." Substantivity is not a subject that underlies accidents (substance), a highly problematic explanation since that subject does not seem to exist in many material realities, but rather a system or constellation of notes or, more precisely, a "primary unit of notes cyclically closed".[31] This approach is original and new and deserves all attention; but even so, it does not appear that it can resolve in a completely satisfactory way the problems posed by the substance. The way in which Zubiri defines substantivity seems to be able, in effect, to avoid the problems of Aristotelian substantialism when we refer to inanimate beings, in which it is very difficult, not to say impossible, to identify that subject (hidden, in addition); but perhaps it increases them if we refer to superior realities that do have a subject. While it seems very adequate to refer to non-living realities as a unitary system in which all the parts are interconnected forming a whole without any of them assuming a decisive priority, it does not seem so much so for living beings that are unitary systems with an activity centralized by a subject (whose status does not interest us for now) which does not appear in Zubiri's proposal.

This possible limit of Zubirian conceptualization has, in our opinion, the same origin as that of Aristotelian categories, namely, trying *to apply the same*

---

1) There is a science of being qua being.

2) Every science refers to a determined being.

3) Being is not a genus." Aubenque, *El problema del ser en Aristóteles*, 188.

[30] "Some time ago I concluded that it was a question of a program – deducing the universal from what is first – that was not achieved because it could not be achieved, that we were before a promise that was not maintained because it was impossible to maintain." Aubenque, *¿Hay que deconstruir la metafísica?* 92.

[31] Zubiri, *Sobre la realidad*, 53.

concept to everything that is real, that is, to construct a universalistic metaphysics. If we generalize by the inferior, we lose by the superior and vice versa. And *no* alternative, no metaphysical proposal with claims of total universality will completely solve the problem. Either it will go too far, or it will fall short.

c) Personalism as First Sectorial Philosophy

We can admit, in any case, that the metaphysical proposals of a universalistic type can provide a set of general notions capable of enlightening the analysis of the real: an in-depth reflection on what unity means, on what constitutes a being as such, or on the structure of causality. But metaphysics *can never again be first philosophy,* that is, *a kind of knowledge through which all knowledge must necessarily pass structurally.* It will be, rather, in fact, *an auxiliary or, if you prefer, a complementary knowledge.* Let us return to the topic of unity. Let us admit that from the universalistic metaphysical perspective, a notion of unity is designed which is flexible enough to be adapted to a wide number of realities. But what would happen if that notion contrasts with what the experience of the unitary reality of the person shows me?[32] If, for instance, it ended up being contradictory with the reality of personal identity or with some of its characteristics. In that case, who should modify their conceptualization: universalistic metaphysics or anthropology? Doubtless, metaphysics, because personal identity is a fact of experience that cannot be questioned by a general concept. Which leads us to one of the most decisive affirmations of this text: *anthropology (and not metaphysics) is the first science when it comes to the person.*[33]

In conclusion, we believe that metaphysics, in its categorial dimension, be it of the type it may be, can never be a first philosophy of a structural type. If, as a first option, we do not admit the possibility of universal structures, the matter

---

[32] Our concept of experience is explained in Chapter 5.

[33] The same occurs with ethics (and with other relevant sciences). "If, therefore, metaphysics wants to say something more about man than it can say about any natural being, then it needs previously that concept of man that opens up to us only through the self-experience of practical reason as the 'good-for-man,' and which is likewise the starting point of ethics. From this we can conclude that neither ethics derives from metaphysics nor vice versa. As philosophical disciplines with their own way of knowing and with certain systematic reflections on reality, they are constituted rather in a strictly reciprocal way, one supporting and illuminating the other. Let us not forget that reality is not structured in accordance with the philosophical disciplines or our academic canon of subject matters." Martin Rhonheimer, "Ragione pratica e verità della soggettività: l'autoesperienza del soggetto morale alle radici della metafisica e della antropología", in L. Romera (ed.), *Ripensare la metafisica* (Rome: Armando, 2005).

falls under its own weight since this metaphysics simply cannot exist. But if, as a second option, we admit that it exists, in this case it does not become a first philosophy either, because these structures, due to their ambiguity and generality, can never be *a compulsory path for the other areas of knowledge*, but rather a *complement* to the analysis that direct experience shows on the subject under consideration: man, science, ethics.

The main *methodological* consequence of all of this is that the metaphysical cascade procedure should be avoided, that is, the contraction of the universal ens to the particular one, or, what is the same, the construction of concepts by *addition* to the ens, or any similar categorization. A more complex procedure is needed, one founded on mutual support between the sciences according to the following scheme, which we call *the atom of the web of knowledge.*[34]

Figure 3.1. Knowledge network atom

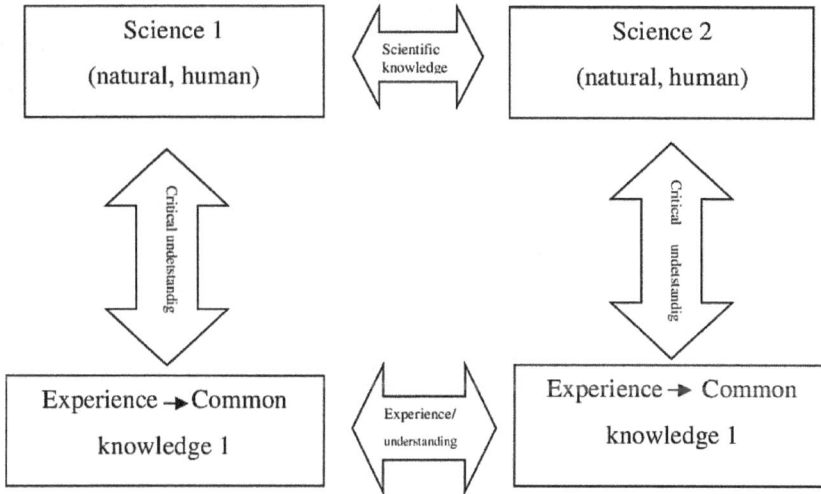

This scheme aims to show that each branch of philosophy starts *from its own core of specific experience* (anthropology, ethics, society) and, through philosophical thought (comprehension and critical comprehension), generates its own field of knowledge. And, since it generates its contents from the *direct* analysis of reality, *this branch of philosophy is first philosophy in its specific field of knowledge because it does not structurally need any other type of mediation to*

---

[34] A detailed explanation of the network of knowledge in J. M. Burgos, *La Fuente originaria. Una teoría del conocimiento* (Granada: Comares 2023).

become a science.[35] And this does not imply any structural or endogamic closure. Every science can and should seek support in connected sciences. Whoever engages in philosophical anthropology should know ethics, psychology, social philosophy, cultural anthropology, and also metaphysics to the extent that it provides knowledge or notions that are useful for the development of anthropology. But the last word in its territory does not depend on other sciences or even on metaphysics. These sciences will provide data, significant relationships, auxiliary concepts, etc. But they cannot modify the structure defined by anthropology (as long as it is sufficiently correct, it is understood) because they do not have sufficient epistemological credentials. Why this happens is evident in the case of similar sciences – ethics, psychology, cultural anthropology. In the case of metaphysics, it follows from all that has been said. There are no universal categories of the real and, in any case, what can be said universally of all beings is of little relevance in terms of their specific identification. Consequently, *anthropology and, therefore, personalism, is a first sectorial philosophy or a first philosophy in its own sphere*, that is, it has the decisive (although not exclusive) word on what pertains to the human person.

---

[35] The analysis can (and should) be fine-tuned depending on the type of knowledge we are referring to. Not all have the same epistemological category.

4

On What Is There: Being and/or Person

It is now time to take on the last pending question, the possible relevance or dependence of the *transcendental order or order of being* (always in the terms elaborated by the metaphysics of being) in relation to anthropology and, in particular, personalism. More concretely, the questions to be posed are the following. Assuming we cannot give universal validity to the Aristotelian categories, *can we or should we continue to consider valid the essence/act of being structure as a constitutive element of all of reality?* If so, what consequences would that have for an anthropology of a personalist type? And if, on the contrary, it were not possible or convenient, would there be an alternative?

4.1 The Essence/Act of Being Structure as Foundation of Reality: Anthropological Implications

Our final objective, as we just indicated, is to attempt to establish whether the dyad act of being/essence can – or should – be taken up by personalist anthropology. An analysis which, logically, we are going to perform from the terms acquired in previous reflections, that is, from the priority granted to anthropology in the study of the human being. Therefore, what we will seek to determine is whether the structure act of being/essence *assists, facilitates, and improves the comprehension of the anthropological phenomenon or not.* And, if not, it would have to be rejected. If, on the contrary, it is shown that this distinction assists in the comprehension of the personal phenomenon in a determined level, its contribution to the illumination of the mystery of the person will be welcomed. But the rules of play are already established. In the same way that anthropology cannot impose overall structures on metaphysics, the contrary is also true: metaphysics cannot impose categories on anthropology that are contradictory to its analyses of human experience.

Having established these premises we can call to mind the essential contents of the metaphysics of being in the transcendental or ontological level: the ens (what exists) is composed of essence and act of being, not in the sense of separable structures, but only as elements or identifiable dimensions of a unitary reality, which is the ens. In each ens, in each thing, we can distinguish the fact of being or existing and what the thing is. Being as act would account for the first aspect, and essence for the second. And, according to Thomism, it is a completely universal distinction, in contrast to the categories, whose universality is relative to their genus. It is not possible, in effect, to escape from this notional duality. The ens, any ens, *is* and, at the same time and necessarily, is *something*: two notions that are limited to distinguishing aspects which in every existing thing occur in a strictly unitary way, since what is real is the ens which is something.

All the entes share this structure, but that does not mean that they are similar. On the contrary, the diversity is manifest, in a gradation which goes from the imperfect material world, through animals, toward personal beings: humans, angels, and God. And it happens that this duality of concepts, in addition to proportioning the essential structure of every ens, can account for the *diversity* through a gradation of act of being and of essence. To every greater perfection there corresponds a greater intensity in the act of being, modulated by a richer and more powerful essence. Until, on the highest level, we find a pure act of being in itself (*Ipsum esse subsistens*), not modulated or limited by any essence, that is, an ens whose own essence is simply to be. The concept of participation allows Thomas Aquinas to thematize this gradation: the different beings participate to a greater or lesser degree in Being. That degree of participation is the essence which limits or modulates the act of being. But participation does not imply that the entes strictly participate in the Being of God. What it signals is that they possess a *limited being* which makes reference to a Being by essence, whose relationship can be explained through the concept of creation. God, Being by essence, creates entes different from Himself which also are, but only in a limited way according to the essence that has been granted to them.

Having presented the central theses of the metaphysics of being on the ontological or transcendental level, the first thing that it seems possible to observe is that this theorization, unlike the Aristotelian categorial structure, *does not present at first sight any negative problem for anthropology*. Accepting that, in the human being, like in the rest of the *entes*, we can distinguish these two dimensions – act of being and essence: being and being human – does not seem to negatively affect any anthropological development, which, it is evident, is due to its *generality*. These notions are so universal that – in contrast to the Aristotelian categories – *they do not imply anything in concrete for any ens. They simply reflect its most basic structure.* Every ens *is something*; a statement – perhaps it is worth the effort to emphasize it – which contributes something more than the mere acknowledgment of the fact that things are given, since it implies the (non-evident) composition of act of being and essence. But, in any case, it seems that one may conclude that an anthropology of a personalist type could take up this structuring of reality without difficulty. In this way, metaphysics, on its ontological level, would contribute to personalism a formal thematization of the fact of being, of existing in the world.

In addition, as we have just seen, metaphysics of being does not just insist on the radical fact of being, but it shows itself to be capable of explaining graduality and diversity through the concept of participation. And, in this framework, it presents the human being as a peculiar and specific being whose essence is situated in a determined place in the cosmos, in the magnificent fan of realities which exist: above and at a great distance from animals, and below and at an infinite distance from God. This vision constitutes, without a doubt, a new and valuable contribution of metaphysics to anthropology by *contextualizing the human being in the world,* something which, from its own idiosyncrasy, as an analysis of the human being and only of the human being, anthropology cannot perform. Metaphysics, on the contrary, thanks to its general character, can gain access to all of reality and this feature assists and illuminates anthropology, indicating to the human being what his place in the cosmos is.

It seems, therefore, that, in the end, *it is possible to establish a positive relationship between metaphysics of being and anthropology* which could be thematized by distinguishing between an *ontological analogy and a categorial analogy,* of which only the first could be taken up by anthropology.[1]

The *categorial analogy* consists in the analogical application of the Aristotelian categories – substance and accidents, act or potency, causality, matter and form, etc. – to the world of the real and, in particular, to anthropology. This analogy, as we have tried to show, does not work correctly in its application to anthropology, but, on the contrary, generates grave problems like the darkening of what is specifically human and its possible deformation.

Ontological analogy would consist in the analogical application of the primary notions of act of being and essence. Every being is a composition of act of being/essence, which can be understood as a limited (by the essence) participation in the Ens which possesses Being in fullness: God. This analogy seems to be compatible with a personalist anthropology.

At this point, one may think that we have reached the close of our investigation, since in the previous chapter we established the relations between metaphysics and personalism on the categorial level and now we have done so on the more radical level, the transcendental one. But it is not so. And

---

[1] I have discovered, with pleasant surprise, through Fabro, that this double consideration of analogy is present in St. Thomas. "Ad secundum dicendum, quod creator et creatura reducuntur in unum, non communitate univocationis sed analogiae. Talis autem communitas potest esse dupliciter. Aut ex eo quod aliqua participant aliquid unum secundum prius et posterius, sicut potentia et actus rationem entis, et similiter substantia et accidens; aut ex eo quod unum esse et rationem ab altero recipit, et talis est analogia creaturae ad creatorem: creatura enim non habet esse nisi secundum quod a primo ente descendit: unde nec nominatur ens nisi inquantum ens primum imitatur; et similiter est de sapientia et de omnibus aliis quae de creatura dicuntur." Thomas Aquinas, *In I Sententiarum,* Prologus, q. 1, a. 2, ad 2.

it is not so because in the previous reflections we have supposed that the notions of act of being and essence describe reality *correctly*. Now, is this so? We will address two important problems in this respect: the possible impersonality of being and, as a consequence, its questionability as an adequate category for reflecting on what exists.

4.2 Is Being Impersonal? On the Possibility of a Personalist Metaphysics

The notion of being (act of being) in Thomas Aquinas implies radically advocating for reality and, more technically, the ens, because it presupposes, implies, or describes that each concretely existing ens (thing, *res*) has a precise act of being and an essence. Up to this point there does not seem to be any problem. It would, at base, be pure realism. But the protagonism of the notion of being in this proposal may present some undesired aspects, in particular, a certain character of impersonality which comes through in the theory of participation and which ends up affecting God. While the theory of the act of being and the essence brilliantly exposes the structure of what exists, it does not make restrictions due to its universality. All realities have a certain degree of being, and the supreme Being has being by essence. Now, *where does the person and the personal stand?* Should this theory insist, in some way, on this aspect or is it unnecessary? But, if this is not performed, does one not run the risk that the vision of God, of the *Ipsum esse subsistens*, will lack the necessary personal character? That it will not be a precise subject, a Someone, but an extremely perfect, but impersonal, being?

Although Scholastic philosophy has *not* insisted on the personal character of God, if one takes up this matter *a posteriori*, it seems like it could be resolved, at least in part, without greater difficulties. If one of the principal features of reality is the personal character, then God should also be a Person by essence, just as he has by essence all the positive qualities of reality. Josef Seifert has taken note of this problem, proposing an interesting solution which consists in taking up the general scheme of the Thomistic ways, but modifying the starting point, which would no longer be things, but the person. If the way starts with a thing or something material, it will only be able to affirm the existence of a super-thing or an impersonal perfection, but *if it starts with a person*, it will lead, with greater or lesser difficulty, but inevitably, to the affirmation of a Person. "*The personalist proofs of the existence of God* proceed in a way similar to the teleological argument – since they too start from the contingent structure of the world of experience – but in a different way than the "cosmological-theological" proofs. They find their starting point in the most elevated of the beings of the cosmos, the person, whose being and essence we experience in ourselves, in order to found from there the existence of God."[2]

It seems, therefore, that this question can be resolved. *There is a path from being or ens to a Personal God.* But the most radical aspect of the problem remains to be solved: *the possible contraposition between being and person.* It occurs that being is not anything concrete, it does not exist as such, it is not an "ens," but rather that by which the ens is. What really exists are the entes as concrete realities: things, vegetables, animals…and persons, who are presented as what is most perfect in the universe. But, if the person is the first and the primary, what is most perfect in the universe, *why is the concept of esse presented as primary in the metaphysics of being, as the founding dimension of reality?* There seems to be here a certain absorption of the person by the *esse,* when being, in itself, is impersonal; it is not someone. A tension which increases to the extent that we go up the ladder of perfection and which leads toward decisive and ultimate questions: *What is more radical, being or the person?* And, *does the person arise from being or does being arise from the Person?*

Thus is posed the problem which could face personalism and metaphysics of being on the ontological level, and which generates a complex area of problematics beyond the synthesis reached in the preceding reflections. Personalism, we said, can take on the structuring of reality into essence and act of being, but, how does this structuring square with the ontological priority of the person? What is primary: being or the person? The matter, there is no need to underscore it, is one of notable complexity. In personalist terms, it seems clear that one would have to affirm that the person is the most radical, inasmuch as the person is abyssmally different from what is non-personal. And, since what is personal cannot arise from what is non-personal, at the peak of reality there should be a personal entity, since, otherwise, it could not create this type of realities. But one could reasonably counter that, although the person is what is most precious in reality, it does not cease to be something that is and, therefore, one must always grant the priority to being, since everything that is, is what it is precisely because it is. But, once again, one could object that,

---

[2] Josef Seifert, *Erkenntnis der Vollkommenen. Wege der Vernunft zu Gott* (Rückersdorf: Lepanto Verlag, 2010), Chapter 4. This path has also been proposed by thinkers like Jacobi: "If reason can exist only in the personality, and if the world has to have a rational, all-moving and governing originator, then this being has to be a Personal being. This being can only be conceived as under the image of human rationality and of personality; to him should be ascribed the qualities of the human being which I consider the most elevated: love, self-consciousness, reason, freedom" (quoted in Bengtsson, *The Worldview of Personalism,* 137).

if the first Ens were not personal, something that does not seem to occur with the Being by essence (or, at least it is not evident, nor is it an essential feature on which metaphysics has insisted), it could not generate personal realities, and therefore that Being must be, from the beginning and in a radical way, personal, that is, a Person. What are the possibilities of resolving this dilemma?

One has the impression that the only viable path should point *toward the radical primacy of a Subsistent Person who would take on, in some way, the contents of the Being by Essence.* A path, moreover, which seems to square well with the Christian perspective, in which there is an identification between Being and Person, an aspect which, however, has not been sufficiently placed in relief in the classical tradition, due to its congenital forgetfulness of the self. In the so-called *Metaphysics of Exodus*, when Yahweh responds to Moses regarding his name, he does not just mention his identification with being, but also offers a *personal* reference: "God said to Moses: '*I* am who I am'. Thus will you say to the Israelites: 'I am' sends me to you" (Ex. 3:14). We are not before the manifestation of an anonymous being, of a subsistent "Being" by essence, or not only: rather, we are before a *Who*, a Someone, a personal Self. It is Someone concrete who responds to that question, not a Perfect but anonymous being. And the same thing happens with Christ. When those convoked by Judas go to arrest him in the Garden of Olives, they have a presentiment of something overwhelming and mysterious, and they stop. Then, Jesus asks them who they seek, and when they respond to him that they are seeking Jesus of Nazareth, he says, "I am." An answer that seems to go beyond a mere factual recognition of his name, because "when he said, "I am," they stepped back and fell to the ground" (Jn. 18:6). Christ seems to be indicating who He really is, affirming an eternally present subsistence or existence, and by saying it, his divine majesty throws to the ground any human power. And what he says is exactly, "I am," an affirmation that is not exactly equivalent to "I am the being by essence" because here the weight of the phrase falls on the *being* while in the first phrase the weight is placed on the personal reality: "I (Christ) am": that is, I am a Personal Subsistent or a Subsistent Person. Is this not the birth of a path which could reconcile traditional metaphysics with the primacy of the Personal reality?[3]

---

[3] The biblical texts are truly suggestive, but it is not possible to base any solid philosophical thesis on them. It is well-known that Gilson advocated for the so-called Metaphysics of Exodus, indicating that, in the passage about the burning bush, God would have proportioned his proper name, which would be precisely that of Being. But, while it is possible to accept that the texts present a certain identification between God and being, which should be taken into account, it is totally impossible to deduce from them a consolidated philosophy, for many reasons. One of them is that the word *hâyâh*, precisely the one used in the expression *'ehyèh 'asher 'ehyèh* (which is normally translated

a) The Classical and Personalist Metaphysics of Josef Seifert

A first possibility within this path would be the classical and personalist metaphysics proposed by Josef Seifert in his work *Essere e persona. Verso una Fondazione fenomenologica de una metafisica classica e personalistica*.[4] Seifert advocates, in the first place, for maintaining a metaphysical structure similar to classical metaphysics or metaphysics of being and, secondly, for eliminating its limitations through a focalization on the person which would lead, for example, to substituting the concept of substance with the concept of person or to pointing toward a Being by essence understood as an "I am" as Final and supreme referent of everything that is given. That is, Seifert, as a prominent representative of phenomenological personalism, clearly notes *the limits of classical metaphysics in its two aspects, categorial and transcendental* and seeks to offer alternatives. On the first level, he indicates that the concept of substance is much poorer than that of subsistence. And, always on the categorial level, he also signals that the theorization of the four causes does not adequately reflect the structure of the personal dynamism, in particular, of freedom, because "in the self-determination of the free subject or of the free substance itself, there is a unique form of causality which is unthinkable within the impersonal being."[5] Along the same lines, he points to the problematic nature of the Aristotelian concept of accident in relation to substance, indicating that "in the case of the person it is clear that the person's being a

---

as "I am who I am") *cannot be identified with the Greek philosophical concept of being* and, in fact, there is no term in the Hebrew vocabulary able to express that idea. The second reason is that the affirmations are so succinct that their interpretation is not clear, a fact even recognized by Gilson, who indicates that it is a question "de la seule formule qui ne dice absolutement rien et qui dice absolutement tout." *L'athéisme difficile* (Paris, 1979), 59. In fact, another of the possible interpretations is that that affirmation is completely negative, that is, that it simply indicates that God does not want to say his name: I am who I am and I do not have a reason to give you explanations about a name. Jean-Luc Marion, *Dieu sans l'être* (Paris: PUF, 2016), 109ff; English version: *God without Being* (University of Chicago Press; Chicago 2012) offers a list of possible explanations of the passage which leaves out the concept of being. Ratzinger, on his part, points toward a more conciliatory position. "The paradox of biblical faith in God is in the union and unity of the two elements we have mentioned; in that being is confessed as person and person as being." J. Ratzinger, *Introducción al cristianismo* (Salamanca: Sígueme, 2005), 115; English: *Introduction to Christianity* (Ignatius Press: San Francisco: 2004).

[4] Josef Seifert, *Essere e persona. Verso una Fondazione fenomenologica de una metafisica classica e personalistica* (Milan: Vita e Pensiero, 1989).

[5] Seifert, *Essere e persona*, 359. The ultimate reason would have to be sought in the fact that Aristotle only noted in a very weak way that the origin of the entire dynamism of efficient causality is freedom.

substance would practically sink into nothingness if it were totally separated from all its accidents."[6]

If we move to the transcendental level, we find a sharp consciousness of the problems that *the impersonal character of being* poses if one sustains its superiority over the concept of person. And he offers his answer in chapter nine of his work, titled "Being is Person," which intends to thematize that personal dimension by describing the reality of being, which leads him, in the last instance, to an integrating proposal between being and person along the lines of the "I am" that we just noted. It seems, therefore, that Seifert's proposal ratifies a good portion of the theses that we have sustained up to now and it implies a step forward along the right line toward establishing a correct balance between metaphysics and personalism.

It seems necessary to us, in any case, to make *two comments*. The first is that Seifert *seems to want to maintain the general structure of the metaphysics of being* and, therefore, he speaks of *classical* and personalist metaphysics, which implies, if our interpretation is correct, that his objective is to maintain the general structure of metaphysics but intensifying its personalist character on its two levels: categorial and transcendental. That is, Seifert does not consider abandoning the universalistic character of traditional metaphysics, but rather *modifying metaphysics in the direction of a universalism capable of satisfactorily integrating the person* through, for example, the substitution of the concept of substance with the concept of person. This path is, doubtlessly, possible, but we have already signaled – and we insist on it again – that, from our point of view, the anthropological value of this universal categorization is small, because it can only contribute a set of very vague and blurry notions. In addition, if one continues to accept the formal structure of classical metaphysics, although modified, one must also accept that anthropology is a second area of knowledge that should be constructed from the starting point of metaphysics. But we have already shown the problems with this position and the correct alternative, in our judgment: there are diverse first areas of knowledge, anthropology is one of them. And metaphysics is, too, but neither of them has absolute primacy; rather, both can and should support each other.

The second aspect that is problematic, or more precisely, unresolved, in Seifert's position has to do with the *non-thematization of the phenomenon of the "I am."* Seifert is fully conscious of the possible impersonal features of the notion of being, and he seeks to resolve them by proposing his "personalization." But, in order for this indication to be operative and not merely consist in a sign that indicates the path to be followed, there needs to be a *much more explicit*

---

[6] Seifert, *Essere e persona*, 379.

thematization of the question. The mere acknowledgment of the priority of the "I am" does not resolve the tension between the concepts of being and person, it simply groups them together, it puts them into contact. We know or intuit that both should be harmonically coordinated among themselves, but the problems do not disappear by affirming it. If the expression or speculative line that points toward the idea of the "I am" sustains the priority of the *Self*, it should explain how this Self appears as a reality that exists (or is) in fact. And if it points to the priority of the I *am*, which does not seem to be the case, one must explain where the person arises from. And, of course, a solution that limits itself to affirming, without further analysis or clarification, the similar value of both is not satisfactory. In conclusion, the synchronous presentation of the concepts sheds light on the solution, but does not offer the solution, so the problem persists.

b) A Non-Categorial Metaphysics of Being

The previous considerations may lead to a proposal that could be more correct and which one might define or describe as *a metaphysics of non-categorial being*, by which we would understand the following:

a)   a metaphysics that takes up the transcendental notions: essence and act of being, participation, etc., but not the Aristotelian categories; that is, a metaphysics exclusively limited to the most radical and ultimate level;

b)   a metaphysics conscious of the value of the person as the primary and primordial reality, and which attempt to draw out the consequences;

c)   a metaphysics that would have ontological priority over anthropology, but which would be subordinate to anthropology in what is relative to the person.

A metaphysics understood in this way would lose a good portion of its old rank as queen of the sciences, but not all of it. It would possess value in itself, as a mode of *overall* interpretation of reality and it would also possess value for anthropology, because *it would situate the human being within the whole of the cosmos*. It would inform anthropology that there are other beings distinct from the person and it would help anthropology to relate with them. In addition, it would not deform or make difficult the comprehension of what is human, as occurs with the Aristotelian categories, because the notions of act of being and essence, due to their generality, do not imply specific anthropological contents.

One could point out that this proposal would resolve the problem of the relation between anthropology and metaphysics fundamentally at the cost of metaphysics, which would be impoverished and minimized in relation to universalist models. And that would not be incorrect. But this appears to be the only acceptable path for overcoming the problems of the universalist visions. And, in addition, these theses could be softened as long as metaphysics elaborates its contents in such a way that they not only are not opposed to the personal character of the human being but serve as a support for that personal character (Polo, Zubiri), in which case, the dialogue between both sciences could be closer and more fruitful. But, in our judgment, the relation between a non-categorial metaphysics of being (more or less extensive) and a personalist anthropology could no longer be established in the terms used in the past, that is, in the terms of classical metaphysics. One could not accept, in any case, an absolute primacy of metaphysics because of the denial of the possibility of a universal, overall categorization, that is, of a categorization capable of establishing with a minimum of precision the specific structures of all entes (things, realities).

A way to formalize this relation would consist in affirming the existence *of a double priority in the relation between metaphysics and anthropology.*

Ontological priority: This would correspond to that science capable of offering the ultimate explanations of the order of *being*. Such a science would be the non-categorial metaphysics of being.

Anthropological priority: This would correspond to the science capable of giving the ultimate explanations about the person. And such a science is anthropology[7] because *metaphysics is in conditions to speak about the person as ens, but not about the person as person,* the latter being the decisive part for its comprehension, since the general affirmations about being (or what is real) only indicate in a very limited way what being a person consists in. In conclusion, *we know what it means to be a person, not thanks to metaphysics, but thanks to anthropology,* just as we know what it means to be good or evil thanks to ethics, not thanks to metaphysics.

From this perspective, therefore, *one could no longer speak of an absolute primacy of one science over another,* neither of anthropology (or ethics) over metaphysics, nor of metaphysics over anthropology or ethics. There would instead be a circular relation of mutual foundation that may be expressed, as we have already indicated, through the *atom of the web of knowledge.*

The atom expresses that there is not an absolutely primary science, but rather, all are related and are interdependent, which does not impede that one or the other could claim priority in a determined area, but never a total and

---

[7] In this context, anthropology and personalism function as equivalent, as long as one takes up a type of anthropology close to the personalist presuppositions. This would not be the case, for example, of an anthropology understood as rational psychology or as metaphysical anthropology in the Thomistic sense.

exclusive priority. Ethics, for example, can claim a radical primacy in its area, considering that it starts from a fact of experience to which it has direct access: moral experience or experience of good and evil and, therefore, it does not depend intrinsically on anthropology. This does not mean, however, that ethics cannot or should not maintain a relation with anthropology, because, if we understand the good as that which perfects the person, we cannot solidly establish what is the good (or the evil) if we do not know in profundity *what the person is*. In conclusion, the autonomy or primacy of ethics in its specific terrain is not total, but sectorial, and it occurs in the context of an interrelationship with anthropology (and with other sciences).[8] In the same way, anthropology can – rightly – demand a primacy in that which specifically concerns the human being. But since it should say at least something about morality or about the social dimension of the subject, it depends on that part of the branches of philosophy that are occupied with those matters. And the same thing happens with metaphysics, with the peculiarity that in this case the relation is established *on a different and more radical plane*, the ontological one. Metaphysics, in effect, does not contribute *specific* data about reality, but rather a general or universal consideration that can help anthropology (or ethics) to better understand itself or to contextualize in relation to the rest of the areas of knowledge or realities.

But – and we insist on this point because the weight of the tradition is very great – that foundation *does not constitute an inevitable and necessary path* through which anthropology and ethics must pass in order to be constituted as sciences. In the first place, because *metaphysics cannot contribute decisive data for understanding the human being*, but only about his place in the cosmos, in addition to some general features of the ens and of the human being as ens. And *none of that defines the person as person* nor is it decisive in the comprehension of the personal being. In summary, *anthropology, in essence, suffices by itself; it is a first science*.

Maintaining this implies sustaining, implicitly, that *an epistemological path exists which can found anthropology (and ethics and the rest of the areas of knowledge)* as a self-consistent science without need of metaphysics; that is, as sciences of the noumenon and of the "thing in itself"; as a radical area of knowledge about man as man. And so it is, in effect. We have denominated this path *integral experience*, and we will address it in the last chapter. We can already anticipate, in any case, that this cognitive path presupposes that experience is the radical principle of all knowledge, including metaphysics; and that the objective of scientific (philosophical) knowledge is to systematize a particular aspect of that knowledge given in experience. In other words,

---

[8] Cf. Rhonheimer, *Ragione pratica e verità della soggettività*, 73-104.

experience is the *original source in which everything real is given*. And, for that very reason, *it is not necessary to pass formally through any science to gain access to what is real, not even to what is real qua real*, since the contents of what exists occur in experience, and the access to experience is universal. It is not metaphysics that evidences the content of what is real, but experience. What metaphysics does, when it does it well, is to formalize, thematize, and make explicit that content. But it does not create it; it does not even discover it. Thus, if anthropology (or ethics) is founded on experience, they can take from there both the content of reality and the specific contents of its subject matter. And, with that, they have more than enough to be consolidated as first sciences in their own area. Subsequently, if they want to and are interested, they will be able to receive a more sophisticated formalization *about reality* offered by metaphysics, that will be able to assist them, if it is well elaborated, to improve their own self-comprehension. And, in the same way, they can receive an interesting and advantageous contextualization of their object in relation to the rest of the existing realities.

Non-categorial metaphysics of being, in conclusion, can be useful for anthropology (or ethics), but always as an auxiliary or complementary knowledge, never as a foundational knowledge.

4.3 Does Being Exist? Toward a Metaphysics of the Ens or of the Real

The possible impersonal character of the notion of being has led toward a metaphysics which, in any of its formulations – categorial (Seifert) or non-categorial – should insist, or at least keep in mind, the priority and primacy of the personal realm. However, none of these options *seems to have been able to resolve in a completely satisfactory way the being-person duality*. Only the proposal of a desired conciliation has been achieved, but there does not seem to be a clear path in this regard. And the reasons for this difficulty are oriented in the direction of the notion of being. The person is a mystery, but, at the same time, the person is an overwhelmingly factual phenomenon. Persons are (we are) there, although it is very difficult to explain what or who we are exactly. But the same thing does not occur with being; rather, the contrary occurs. Being is a very difficult notion to apprehend, even to think about. Within the realist tradition, the centuries-long insistence on being, especially from Thomas Aquinas on, has granted it a certain tone of evidence, in fact. *It is* indisputable and irrefutable that things *are*, a fact that language itself seems to confirm through the predicamental structure which is constructed on the verb *is*. But things are not so simple. Not only has there been a multitude of debates about the exact meaning of the term being *within the Thomistic school*, but the value and even the very existence of being as such has been questioned recently (Marías, Zubiri, Marion, Levinas). Could it not happen, in effect, that we do not find a solution to the dilemma between being and person because it is incorrectly posed? Must be not *rethink the concept of being* in order to avoid this paradox? Must we not even *dispense with the concept of being* and explain reality through other notions that do not lead to this insolvable contradiction? In conclusion, *does being really exist?* Or, on the contrary, should this concept be abandoned and substituted by another one, which would be able to help in resolving the problems which we face?

We are fully conscious of the significance and transcendence of this question. And we do not intend to resolve it in a few pages. Our objective is more limited and is framed within the context of this investigation: to arrive at the base of the relation between personalism and metaphysics, which implies analyzing the question of being in order to evaluate whether it is *an adequate concept for anthropology* or whether, on the contrary, there are indications that its position or weight in the interpretation of reality should be rethought. And, in order to center such a vast topic, we will take as our basis the reflections of Jean-Luc Marion and Xavier Zubiri.

a) God Without Being, According to Marion: The Question of Ontotheology

We are going to follow Marion's analysis as it is proposed in his work *God without Being* which in its very title already poses the problem that we want to analyze. Marion starts with the Heideggerian conception of being which takes form in his ontotheological proposal in which being is constituted as the final foundation of all reality and which Heidegger himself defines in these terms: "The ontotheological constitution of metaphysics proceeds from the potency of difference, which maintains, separate and at the same time united, being as foundation (*Sein als Grund*) and ens as that which is founded (*Seiendes als gegründet*) and at the same time as founder (*begründendes*), a connection which assures the conciliation (*Austrag*)."[9]

An affirmation which means, principally, three things:

1) That being founds every ens as being the being of the ens.

2) That, by logical consequence, it also founds God as ens, since in order to be Ens, he must (first) be.

3) That God or the supreme Ens is responsible for the efficient causation of the entes, which is not an obstacle for his being founded, in turn, by being.

---

[9] Martin Heidegger, *Die onto-theologische Verfassung der Metaphysik*, in *Identität und Differenz* (Pfullingen, 1957), 63. Quoted in Jean-Luc Marion, *Dieu sans l'être*, 283.

That is, *the ontological difference* distinguishes the ens (what exists) from being (as foundation), but it grants a radical priority to being, because it founds that which is founded (the ens) which is, therefore, second. Thus the famous call of Heidegger urging the *recuperation of being*, the primary and first reality, versus the traditional Western insistence on the ens.

It does not seem difficult to intuit that the precise and potent Heideggerian vision of being harbors some of the problems that we have noted in this notion. Levinas, for example, has denounced its radically impersonal character which, in some way, we had already detected in Thomistic metaphysics: "To affirm the priority of *being* with respect to the *ens*, is already to pronounce on the essence of philosophy, to subordinate the relation with *someone* who is an ens (ethical relation) to a relation with *the being of the ens* which, impersonal, allows the apprehension, the domination of the ens."[10]

Marion, in line with Levinas, detects that this problem affects God, that in the (Heideggerian) ontotheology, is nothing other than *a particular case of the ens* and, since the ens is founded by being, the same thing occurs with "God," even if this "God" possesses a causative or founding mission on the level of the ens. "God," in this context, cannot be anything other than a mere gear of metaphysics, concretely, the piece which metaphysics needs in order to close the internal chain which connects entes to each other, but always on the second level of the ens. Therefore, and depending on which metaphysics one is speaking of, God could be causa sui, unmoved Mover, or whatever is convenient or necessary in each system, but always and in every case, he will be at the service of metaphysics and *at the orders of being*; he will be a mere link (although the principal one) in the chain of entes whose final foundation is *being*. And this god, as Heidegger himself recognized, cannot be praised, nor worshipped, nor sung to. It is hardly a transcendent god; at most a god of the philosophers; not a personal god and much less a god of faith, because it could be that, in reality, it is not God at all.

Marion considers that this criticism cannot be overcome in the Heideggerian world, which would imply that the notion of being – incompatible with the transcendence of God – *should be abandoned*. But, conscious that proposing the abandonment of being in the framework of the realist tradition and of "Christian philosophy" is no small matter, since this notion has been considered

---

[10] Emmanuel Levinas, *Totalidad e infinito*, 5th ed. (Salamanca: Sígueme, 2002), 59 and more in general, "La metafísica precede la ontología," 66-71. English: *Totality and Infinity: An Essay on Exteriority* (Pittsburgh, Pa.: Duquesne University Press, 1969). See also Emmanuel Levinas, *De la existencia al existente* (Madrid: Arena Libros, 2006) where he affirms the primacy of the existent over existence, which points, although with another terminology, to the primacy of the ens over being.

the last fortress against the relativistic challenges, he takes a step back to ask: should Thomas Aquinas' vision of being also be framed within ontotheology? Or, on the contrary, would it escape this criticism? Because, if the latter were the case, perhaps it would not be necessary to adopt such a radical measure as the abandoning of being, since the problems of ontotheology would not affect the Metaphysics of being and the Thomistic *actus essendi*.

Marion has analyzed this question profoundly in the article *Saint Thomas d'Aquin et l'onto théo-logie*,[11] which will be the basis of our reflections.

The first thing Marion notes is that Thomas Aquinas' position is complex, in contrast to other Scholastics or post-Thomists, like Scotus and, above all, Suárez, who did not have a problem with considering God as an object or topic of metaphysics. Thus, the question should be studied in detail and with subtlety in order to not fall into erroneous conclusions.[12] Aquinas, in effect, shows himself to be reluctant to consider God as an object of metaphysics and always distinguishes between "metaphysical theology" and *sacra doctrina*, which lies outside metaphysics (and deals with God without difficulty). The basis of these nuances is constituted by Thomas Aquinas' sharp consciousness of the radical diversity of God and, in consequence, of the intrinsic limitations of philosophy to adequately deal with Him. One only reaches God "on tiptoes," so to speak, and as the principle of all that exists, not directly, which puts into question whether God can be, point blank, an object of metaphysics like others. "Philosophers, then, study these divine beings only insofar as they are the principles of all things. Consequently, they are the objects of the science that investigates what is common to all beings"[13] In conclusion, in confrontation with Scholastics like Suárez, who advocates for an ontotheology obviously not understood in a strictly Heideggerian sense, but who accepts that God as an ens is an object of metaphysics, Thomas is much more cautious in this regard, noting that God is a principle of metaphysics, but that he does not allow himself to be completely captured by it.

----

[11] The article was originally published in *Revue thomiste* (XCV, 1 1995) and republished with some minimal modifications in Jean-Luc Marion, *Dieu sans l'être*, 279-332.

[12] In fact, this is what happened to Marion, who included Thomas Aquinas within ontotheology in the first edition of *Dieu sans l'être* and, in the article that we are going to comment on, he corrects this error.

[13] Thomas Aquinas, *In Boetii De Trinitate*, lect. II, q. 5, a. 4: "Res divinae non tractantur a philosophis, nisi prout sunt rerum omnium principia. Et ideo pertractantur in illa doctrina, in qua ponuntur ea quae sunt communia omnibus entibus." English text: Joseph Kenny, "St. Thomas Aquinas's Works in English," April 5, 2022, https://isidore.co/aquinas/Boethius DeTr.htm/.

This is the framework within which Thomas distinguished *two different types of* being: the *esse commune* (proper to creatures) and the *esse divinum.* "God's being which is his essence is not universal being, but being distinct from all other being."[14] "Nor is it necessary, if we say that God is existence alone, for us to fall into the error of those who say that God is universal existence whereby each and every thing formally exists. For the existence which God is, is such that no addition can be made to it. Whence by virtue of its purity it is an existence distinct from every existence."[15]

What can be deduced from such suggestive and notable texts? Above all, that Thomas Aquinas remains outside of ontotheology since he denies the double foundation between being and ens; that is, universal being does not found God, since, in some way, *there are two classes of "being (esse),"* common being, proper to creatures, and divine being.[16] There is nothing like universal, infinite and, therefore, impersonal being over which everything real would be constituted (Heidegger). God exists with his own being, the being of the *ipsum esse subsistens,* in which the essence is not differentiated from being. And the *esse commune* of creatures exists, which is a different *esse.* Along similar lines, Thomas denies that God is *causa sui* (against the postulates of ontotheology) because, in addition to the logical oxymoron (which has no theoretical relevance), he never conceives God as one more ens among others, subjected to the general rules of entes. God is radically different: he only causes and is not caused. There is no type of reciprocity between entes and God, nor, therefore, dependence. Nor is his causality only efficient, as Descartes thinks, but rather it takes on all the levels of causality. In summary, for Marion, Thomas Aquinas remains outside ontotheology, but with this condition: "if, by chance, God had

---

[14] Thomas Aquinas, *De potentia* VII, a. 2, ad 4: "Esse divinum, quod est eius substantia, non est esse commune, sed est esse distinctum a quolibet alio esse." English text: Joseph Kenny, "St. Thomas Aquinas's Works in English," April 5, 2022, https://isidore.co/aquinas/QD dePotentia7.htm.

[15] Thomas Aquinas, *De ente et essentia* IV: "Nec oportet, si dicimus quod Deus est esse tantum, ut in illorum errorem incidamus, qui Deum dixerunt esse illud esse universale, quo quaelibet res formaliter est. Hoc enim esse, quod Deus est, huius condicionis est, ut nulla sibi additio fieri possit; unde per ipsam suam puritatem *est esse distinctum ab omni esse.*" English text: Joseph Kenny, "St. Thomas Aquinas's Works in English," April 5, 2022, https://isidore.co/aquinas/DeEnte&Essentia.htm. (The emphasis is ours.)

[16] "The *esse commune* designates, so to speak, the first placing into act of creatures, that is, that the act of *esse* unfolds in creatures and essences which it actualizes according to the respective natures and degrees of their perfection." Fabro, *Participación y causalidad,* 332. "This *esse commune* is not an abstract formality nor a single act of being common to all beings, but the *actualitas essendi,* which every being receives through the intermediation of its own *esse,* participated of God." Ibid., 333.

to be, he would never be as a part of the object (or the subject) of *metaphysica*, nor above all according to a univocal concept of *ens* (*étant*)."[17]

That is, Thomas Aquinas remains outside of ontotheology as long as one accepts that he possesses *a concept of being that is, in a certain sense, equivocal* which differentiates in a very profound way the *esse commune* from the *Ipsum esse*. This is the price one must pay, according to Marion, to free Thomas from ontotheology. If being is present as a relatively unitary reality, it becomes the primary concept, absorbing God within its interior (Heidegger) and converting him into one of its objects, one of the entes which it founds, as decisive as this particular ente may be in the entitative order. But if, on the contrary, one accepts the heterogeneity of being, does the Thomistic proposal not become radically altered?

This is the problem. A complicated problem which the traditional notions of analogy do not seem to be in a condition to resolve.[18] In particular, it does not seem that the analogy of proportionality is able to do it, because analogous participation in being can never be understood as a greater or lesser possession of the same thing, because the divine Being is *different* from any other being: "est esse distinctum a quolibet alio esse." Thus, Marion suggests the solution of the "focal point," a modern version of analogy which can be applied when there is a group of objects that share a type of reality that the principal possessor possesses in a radically different way from the others, which brings with it a

---

[17] Marion, *Dieu sans l'être*, 300.

[18] In Thomism there is a classic debate in this regard, represented by Cajetan and Suárez. For the former, the ens would have an analogy of proper proportionality; for the latter, an analogy of intrinsic attribution. González Álvarez, who has studied the debate, has his own intermediate position: he says Suárez is correct with regard to the essence (*ens ut nomen*) and Cajetan is correct with regard to the existence (ens as participle): "It corresponds to the essences to be in themselves more or less perfect and to situate themselves vertically in a determined degree and hierarchy. Graduated participation of existence has its root in this. But the analogy of intrinsic attribution implies that verticality and graduation in the realization of the analogous form. Thus the ens as a noun should be analogous with analogy of intrinsic attribution. The ens as participle designates an existence to which it corresponds to be under a determined modality. The existence expressed by it directly is, in itself, ungraduable. Something exists or does not exist, but it does not exist more or less. Here there is no order of prior and posterior; there is no rank or hierarchy. The previous verticality cedes its place to the strictest horizontality. This is precisely what the analogy of proper proportionality demands." González Álvarez, *Tratado de Metafísica*, 186. An expansion of the topic in Rafael Díaz, "La analogía," in Francisco Fernández Labastida and Juan Andrés Mercado (eds.), *Philosophica: Enciclopedia filosófica online*, URL: <http://www.philosophica.info/archivo/2010/voces/analogia/Analogia.html>.

certain incommensurability and unintelligibility. Which is just what occurs between the elements which remit to a focus and the focus itself.[19]

In any case, and beyond the search for a theory that might explain these phenomena, the central question which this perspective generates is that the abandonment of the comfortable – but not very precise – analogy *puts into question the traditional version of the concept of being.* Is it admissible to integrate everything that exists, including God, into a notion that presents itself with features of equivocity? Some Thomists have supported Marion's interpretation or have sustained it independently, like Aubenque.[20] And there are texts of Thomas Aquinas that justify it. "'To be' can mean either of two things. It may mean the act of essence, or it may mean the composition of a proposition effected by the mind in joining a predicate to a subject. Taking "to be" in the first sense, we cannot understand God's existence nor His essence; but only in the second sense."[21] But other Thomists, like Gilson, consider that, even accepting the existence of that difference, it is not necessary to establish such a radical rupture. God is a very different Being, *but he is Being,* and he himself, in the Metaphysics of Exodus, gave himself that name. Therefore, "the name of onto-logy does not go well with Thomistic metaphysics, because it consists more in a consideration of being than in a discourse about the ens"[22] and should look with sympathy to Heidegger, who has once again brought the primary question of being to the philosophical gaze.[23]

---

[19] The tension in the concept of participation between the similarity between beings and the dissimilarity with God has been recognized by some Thomists. Cf. Cornelio Fabro, *Participación y causalidad,* 472ff.

[20] Cf. P. Aubenque, *El problema del ser en Aristóteles,* 169, 175 and passim.

[21] Thomas Aquinas, *S. Th.* I, q. 3, a. 4, ad 2: "Esse dupliciter dicitur, uno modo, significat actum essendi; alio modo, significat compositionem propositionis, quam anima adinvenit coniungens praedicatum subiecto. Primo igitur modo accipiendo esse, non possumus scire esse Dei, sicut nec eius essentiam, sed solum secundo modo." English text: Joseph Kenny, "St. Thomas Aquinas's Works in English," April 5, 2022, https://isidore.co/aquinas/summa/FP/FP003.html.

[22] Etienne Gilson, *L'être et l'essence,* 1948, 372 (quoted by Jean-Luc Marion, *Dieu sans l'être,* 317). Along similar lines, Eudaldo Forment summarizes Thomas Aquinas' entire theory with the expression: "order of being." Cf. St. Thomas Aquinas, *El orden del ser. Antología esencial* (coord. E. Forment) (Madrid: Tecnos, 2003). And Vittorio Possenti titles his last work, in which he proposes a return to metaphysics, *Ritorno all'essere. Addio alla metafisica moderna* (Rome: Armando Editore, 2019).

[23] The similarities between Gilson and Heidegger (although the differences as well) have been underscored by Aubenque, *¿Hay que deconstruir la metafísica?*

In sum, and preparing to leave behind Thomas Aquinas' thought, Marion concludes, in a very nuanced way, the following[24]:

1. Thomas Aquinas remains essentially outside ontotheology as Heidegger defines it;

2. At the same time, he is one of those who have done more to consolidate *metaphysica* (and even ontotheology) by including God in the concept of being, introducing a radical course change with respect to previous Christian tradition. Because up until Thomas, in effect, a good portion of Christian thought, along more Platonic lines, did not make being an absolute priority, but rather did so with the good or some other of the divine names. It is Thomas who, due to the Aristotelian influence, establishes the priority of being, including God in it. And although he does so with all the previously mentioned nuances, one could say that he is the one principally responsible, in a much greater degree than Suárez, for the advent of ontotheology.

3. Finally, and beyond all these considerations of a more exegetical type, Marion considers that the concept of being is not adequate for "explaining" God, but *rather it should be God who explains being*, which would place this notion in a secondary and significantly distinct situation from the one adopted by Thomas Aquinas in any of his interpretations. In fact, it is the posture which Christianity has adopted for a long time, and it is the posture that he explores in his book with an unequivocal title: *God without being*.

In the realm of propositions (more complex than the realm of critique), Marion's alternative proposals go by "theological" paths and intend to be founded on specifically Christian features elaborated from texts of revelation which point toward *a call or relationship with God in which it would not be important whether things are or are not*, like this text from Romans 4:17: "I have placed you as a father of many peoples before God, in whom he believed, who gives life to the dead *and calls things that are not as if they were*."[25] And, above all, the presence of the gift and *charitas*, as a instance previous to being: "Charity delivers Being/ens."[26] That is, Marion opens up to the existence of a superior and first order from which the order of being/ens would arise, although he is fully conscious of the enormous difficulty which establishing its

---

[24] Marion, *Dieu sans l'être*, 318.

[25] The emphasis is ours. Other texts are 1 Cor. 1:28 and the parable of the prodigal son, Lk. 15:12-32.

[26] Marion, *Dieu sans l'être*, 148.

characteristics brings with it: "To specify how the distance determines Being/ens without intrinsically affecting it would require a specific study, whose difficulty detains us. What is important here is to signal this acquisition alone: Biblical revelation offers, in a few texts, the flowering of a certain indifference of the ens with respect to Being."[27]

b) From Being to Ens, to the Real Concrete Existent

Marion's analysis is very suggestive, and its principal merit, in our judgment, resides in posing a series of difficulties around the notion of being which oblige us to go beyond a lackadaisical vision, according to which, through the notions of participation and analogy, one could consistently, precisely, and clearly explain the structure of reality. Marion's central thesis, which points toward the need to accept a certain equivocity in being as the only way to not fall into ontotheology, the submission of God to metaphysics, annuls this perspective. The concept of being becomes more problematic than expected and it advocates for new solutions. Now, the alternatives proposed by the French philosopher are not particularly convincing. His principal proposal, recourse to *agape/charitas*, as the primary element of reality, has a solid basis in the newness of Christian Revelation (God is love), but its theoretical interlocking is complex. Is it possible to consider the first principle as gift, when that first principle is only a relational concept? Should one not start with a self-referential concept in the identification of what is First, or at a minimum, should that principle not contain the self-referential dimension? These are extremely interesting questions, but we must go back in order to reach some kind of conclusion.

Up to now, we have the following: the notion of being has been considered decisive within the framework of realist philosophy (and Christian thought), but, although it has some very valuable features, it also seems to present significant problems: the possible drift toward ontotheology; a certain impersonal character; the difficulties in explaining the differentiation between the *esse commune* and the *Ipsum esse*, understood as different types of being, etc. And it is natural to think that these problems will influence anthropology if one accepts that every ens is a composite of essence and act of being, and that the primacy in that composition corresponds to being which is act. Since anthropological reflection does not begin with being, one may think that that influence will be weak and distant, but one should not underestimate the power of concepts. If philosophy establishes a primacy of being, and that concept is problematic or its boundaries have not been satisfactorily defined,

---

[27] Marion, *Dieu sans l'être*, 147.

the problems, sooner or later, will come. Is there a solution in this regard, beyond Marion's proposal?

A possible path of solution is the following: what would happen if, maintaining the notion of being, we opted for *a primacy of the ens*? Would there not be a possibility of finding there a path for the solution of the problems posed? Would the difficulties that derive from placing in a preferential place a "being" which, in reality, "is" not, that is to say, which does not exist as such, with the exception of the *Ipsum esse*, not dissolve in some way, since what really exists are *entes*?

Opting for the primacy of the ens does not seem, at first sight, to be a very brilliant or fitting decision since, from the start, we find Zubiri's harsh criticism of the "entification of reality" which Scholasticism seems to have performed; that is, the transformation or subsumption of reality into the *concept* of ens, thus substituting the real world with the conceptual world. We have no difficulty agreeing with Zubiri and recognizing that, with a certain frequency, Scholasticism – especially in its less brilliant versions – has ended up identifying what is real with the concept of ens from which, by contraction (or addition, depending on how you look at it), everything real would be derived. We have already seen this. But, to be fair with Scholasticism and, in particular, with Thomas Aquinas, it seems that one may also recognize *in the notion of ens an important area of concern for realists which should be considered attentively.* When Thomas Aquinas affirms that, "the first thing that the understanding conceives, as that which is most known, and in which it resolves all its other concepts, is the ens... Thus, it is necessary that all the other concepts of the understanding be taken by addition to the ens,"[28] it is clear that, to some extent, he moves toward the world of the *concept* of ens and its determinations and toward the entification denounced by Zubiri.[29] But it is also true, and cannot be denied, that this expression indicates that the understanding begins its work with *what exists, that is, that which is, that is, the ens.* And not with being. The nuance is decisive. In the texts in which Thomas refers to the beginning of knowledge, he does not mention being, but the ens. And, therefore, both terms cannot simply be identified.[30] The Thomistic texts, repeatedly and with precision, do not affirm this; they do not sustain that thought begins from

---

[28] Thomas Aquinas, *De veritate*, q. 1, a. 1, resp.

[29] Cf. Zubiri, *Los problemas fundamentales de la metafísica occidental*, 105.

[30] As occurs, for example, in this text: "For Thomas Aquinas, the beginning of thought is the ens, that is, 'that which is' (*id quod est*), that which exercises the act of being. *Thought, therefore, unfolds from the consciousness of being*, that is, after the primordial observation of 'what is in the process of being' [*lo que está siendo*]." C. Benavides, "El ser en Tomás de Aquino desde la perspectiva de Cornelio Fabro," in *Azafea. Revista filosófica*, 16 (2014), 111-131; (the emphasis is ours).

being, nor do they sustain that it begins from the concept or notion of ens; what they affirm is that, in the beginning, *the ens* is there.[31] Therefore, the ens, and not being, is first. Being does not give meaning to the ens, as occurs in Heidegger, but just the opposite, the ens gives meaning to being. Being does not accept, found, and give meaning to the ens, because it cannot do so, since we only find being in the ens, which is what really exists. And we are not referring, of course, to the *concept* of ens, but to the real ens, that is, the *really existing thing* represented, indeed, through the concept or notion of ens, since philosophy cannot but express itself through concepts, even if it wants to refer to what is most individual.

One has the impression, therefore, that a certain priority of the ens over being could, at least to some extent, be accepted in the doctrine of Thomas, which would justify – within the framework of this tradition – that *option for the ens over and above being*, which, moreover, is in exquisite syntony with the central nucleus of this philosophy: realism, fidelity to what exists just as it is shown to the intellect. And what is shown to the intellect is, above all, the ens, that which is concretely given, and not being, whose intellection, justification, and interpretation are difficult. What is evident are things, what is given there, what there is, while being is always and only given as a dimension or interpretation of the ens, without an independent existence, except in the case of the *Ipsum esse*, to which, moreover, we can only approach in a purely inferential way.

What happens, then, if one opts for this primacy of the ens? Perhaps what happens is that we would find the beginning of a solution to some of the problems that have been posed. In the framework of a primacy of the ens, the possibility of a fall into ontotheology disappears, since being loses its foundation primacy. In the same way, the disparity between the *esse commune* and the *Ipsum esse* ceases to be so problematic, since *being only appears as a dimension of the ens*, while the diversity of the ens becomes clear, perhaps even more so than its unity. That the being which inhabits in such diverse entes is also diverse is logical and natural. Finally, the problem of the possible impersonal character

---

[31] "Illud enim quod primo acquiritur ab intellectu est ens, et id in quo non invenitur ratio entis non est capibile ab intellectu." Thomas Aquinas, *In librum De Causis*, lect. 6. "Illud autem quod primo intellectus conceipit quasi notissimum, et in quod conecptiones omnes resolvit, est ens." Thomas Aquinas, *De veritate*, q. 1, a. 1, resp. "Primum enim quod cadit in imatination intellectus, est ens, sine quo nihil potest apprehendi ab intellectu." Thomas Aquinas, *In I Sententiarum*, d. 8, q. 1, a. 3. "Intellectus autem per prius apprehendit ipsum ens; et secundario apprehendit se intelligere ens; et tertio apprehendit se appetere ens. Unde primo est ratio entis." Thomas Aquinas, *S. Th.*, I, q. 16, a. 4, ad 2. Our understanding is that this is the correct interpretation of St. Thomas but, in any case, it is the position which seems most adequate to us.

of being also seems to weaken. As soon as being ceases to be the reference point, which we transfer to the ens, the access to or revelation of what is personal does not pose so many problems. It is enough to distinguish between those entes that are not persons and those that are, and which spontaneously become manifest as a "who," something which does not occur with being, always surrounded by a nimbus of impersonality. In conclusion, the option for *the primacy of the ens*, with the consequent replacement of being on a second level, seems to resolve some of the problems which we have encountered.

This solution, if viable, would bring with it a certain devaluation of the concept of being within the Thomistic tradition where it may have been overvalued. Both Gilson and Fabro, for example, fascinated by the Thomistic (re)discovery of the *esse ut actus* or "intensive being," have insisted, correctly and meritoriously, on the first and primary character of being, in its superiority over essence. And, in that sense, Fabro signals that "the supreme act by which every other act is in act, substantial or accidental, is the *esse*, which is the proper and immediate effect of God."[32] Now, does this very sentence not show that excess around being? What is really the effect of creation, the *esse* or the real thing? It thus seems, against Gilson,[33] that Thomistic metaphysics could – and perhaps should – be called metaphysics of the ens or *ontology*, understood as a treatise on the ens, and not a metaphysics of being.[34]

c) A Metaphysics of the Real. A Reflection about Zubiri

This path seems promising, but what happens is that the notion of ens is very much marked by history and inseparably linked to Scholastic philosophy. Thus, an appeal to the ens could easily be misinterpreted, in the sense in which it was criticized by Zubiri, giving the impression that what one seeks is to begin with

---

[32] Fabro, *Participación y causalidad*, 331.

[33] Etienne Gilson, *L'être et l'essence*, 1948, 372 (quoted in Jean-Luc Marion, *Dieu sans l'être*, 317).

[34] The consideration of God as ens from this perspective does not seem problematic, that is, no more problematic than any other consideration of the divine may be. To affirm that God is an ens would simply mean that God exists, is there or is something. Determining What or Who that God is a very different question and difficult to resolve. But, certainly, it should not be done through the general categories of the ens, since then we would fall back into ontotheology. It is true that Thomas Aquinas refers to God on numerous occasions as the first ens, but this expression does not pose problems if we apply to it the same considerations as Marion regarding being. God is certainly the *First ens* in the sense that he is something that exists and is real, a concrete and specific being. But God is not just another ens (or thing), but rather an ens which is transcendentally above any ens or reality and, therefore, not subject to its laws. From this interpretation, there is not, in our judgment, any problem with treating God as the Supreme Ens, the First Ens or, simply, an ens.

an abstract general concept as an expression of what is real and singular, when the pretension is just the opposite. In addition, it would be very complex – not to say impossible – to distinguish the notion of ens from the complex elaboration of the metaphysics of being which takes it as the key and primary point of the entire Aristotelian-Thomistic categorial structure: substance and accidents, matter and form, teleology, etc. In the end, the notion of ens has been forged within this tradition and it would be a semantic utopia to try to isolate a part from the whole, accept the notion of ens and simply abandon the rest. Thus, although from the perspective we are suggesting the notion of ens (understood as thing/ *res*) could be recuperable, it seems reasonable to pose a *semantic* alternative, free from that enormous conceptual inertia. Happily, we can count on valid candidates such as reality, the real, what there is (*lo que hay*), since, in effect, ens, according to the definition that we are accepting here, is nothing but just that: what is real, what is there, what is given, what is absolutely primary.[35]

Doubtless, here we are very close to Zubiri, whose metaphysics consists of an investigation about *what is real*, a notion with which he intends to overcome the entification of what is given or factual and return thought to the world of the concrete existent. In fact, one may find in Zubiri a criticism of the notion of being which is similar to that of Marion. Zubiri questions the absolute need for this notion, indicating that its supposed universality is not even semantic, because there are languages that do not use the verb to be, to say nothing of the expressions, with the languages that do use the verb to be, which remit to existence without employing the verb to be. In Spanish: *lo que hay* or *hay cosas*; *il y a*, in French. In that direction, the nucleus of his position consists in the attempt to found a realism in which the concept of being is not as relevant as in the classical tradition. And, in this context, Zubiri opts for the line that we are indicating: an option for the real, for the factually given, for things or what exists as the starting point of thought and, therefore, of philosophy.[36]

Philosophy starts with raw or naked reality, which is characterized "by being in itself," which means that "whatever may be the thing with all its moments and the articulation of them, these pertain to the thing *in* itself and they are not expended simply in the moment in which the impression affects one."[37] Zubiri expresses here, together with his "ontological" option for what is real, the basic

---

[35] The term "thing" would also appear to be valid. However, its recent philosophical use has restricted it to the realm of the non-personal, as when one affirms that the person is not a thing. Thus, its use as a universal has become problematic.

[36] As we saw, Marion's path diverges on this point, pointing along the lines of the *ágape*. The Zubirian line seems more convincing to us.

[37] Zubiri, *Sobre la realidad*, 27.

epistemological principle of realism: what is given, because it is in itself, is not exhausted in the moment of its perception, be it through the impression or, much more generally, through the sentient intelligence. And, in this way, he manages to *affirm reality without having recourse to being*. One verifies, affirms, and recognizes what there is (*lo que hay*), but without the need for being to intervene. One does not affirm that things are, although this is not denied. More still, in fact, Zubiri uses the notion of being, but in a second moment, once the real has led the way affirming itself as "in itself". Thus he affirms, in terms very similar to those we are sustaining here, that "what we call ens is purely and simply reality in its being. There is not *esse reale*, real being, but rather *realitas in essendo*, reality in being. Every reality, then, inasmuch as it is actual in the world, has this that we call being,"[38] which is, for Zubiri, a type of reaffirmation of the thing over itself. "The actuality of a substantive reality in that respectivity envelops a type of reaffirmation, if you will, or ratification of what substantive reality is with respect to other things. That ratification is what we call *being*."[39]

What we have said is enough, since we do not intend to enter into the complex Zubirian metaphysics. But we do want to add a concluding consideration. While we highly value Zubiri's position with respect to the question of being and his option for the primacy of the real, we cannot pass over the fact that one of his great objectives has been to construct *a universalist metaphysics that would be an alternative to the metaphysics of being*. Zubiri understood in depth the limits of traditional metaphysics; its difficulties in adequately dealing with the person, the deficiencies in the concept of substance, etc. And he designed an alternative metaphysics *that knew beforehand the pitfalls that were to be avoided*. Thus, he distinguished between what he calls closed essence and open essence, which allows him to adequately gain access to the notion of person, since the open essence, in the end, is nothing other than the person.[40] It is an intelligent approach which is very much on the mark, but which remits, once again, to our key question: Should the renewed Zubirian metaphysics be *an obligatory step for anthropology?* And once again we respond, no. The pretension of establishing some valid categories for all that is real continues to seem unacceptable. In fact, the mention we have made of the notions of open essence and closed essence has

---

[38] Zubiri, *Sobre la realidad*, 158.

[39] Zubiri, *Sobre la realidad*, 231.

[40] "The greatest good that God has created in the world is that of an essence which defines its reality with respect to itself; which is free, if you will. […] It is this character, in virtue of which we say that the human essence is its own, to which we refer when we express that the human being is a person." Zubiri, *Sobre la realidad*, 203 and 209ff.

just that purpose, because *Zubiri already knows what a person is when he elaborates these concepts*. And, thus, he elaborates them in such a way that when, in his passage through reality, he has to account for the human (or divine) person, he may do so correctly. But this does not mean anything but that *the person does not arise from metaphysics, but rather is previous to it*. Zubiri does not construct anthropology under the dictates of metaphysics, but, at least to some extent, he does the opposite. He constructs a metaphysics that can adequately and satisfactorily account for personal being because he defines his concepts in relation to a *previous anthropology*. On occasion, as in the case of open and closed essence, these concepts may work (although one would have to analyze whether the distinction generates equivocity in the concept of essence), but in others, like that of substantivity,[41] the same thing does not occur, in our judgment. Therefore, it seems that not even in the renewed metaphysics of Zubiri is it possible to opt for an authentic and *strict universalist metaphysics*, but rather for a mutual influence between areas of knowledge along the lines of the atom of the web of knowledge.

We conclude: 1) while the Thomistic thematization of what is real does not strictly imply a primacy of being in this philosophy, a prevalence of this dimension with respect to the dimension of the ens has frequently occurred in practice, which leads one to describe God as *Ipsum esse* and creatures as *entes* which participate in the being of God; 2) this primacy of being, with all its positive aspects, presents relevant problems as well, such as the possible fall into ontotheology from which one could only exit by accepting a certain equivocity of being (*esse commune, Ipsum esse*), difficult to justify on the basis of analogy or participation; the possible impersonal character of being, etc.; 3) but if one opts for the primacy of the ens (thing, *res*), which seems possible according to the realist presuppositions of Thomas Aquinas, perhaps these problems could be obviated inasmuch as the ens is always something concrete and specific which can be a person; 4) in this way, the ascending path would not lead only to Being by Essence, but to a singular and determined Ens which, logically, could not be Something, but Someone, that is, a Personal Ens; 5) finally, from this perspective, creation should not be understood as a segmentation of the infinite ocean of Being into little parts which the concretes entes would be, but as the placing into reality of the multiplicity of what exists from the starting point of a Subsistent Person.

The metaphysics which would take on these presuppositions – which are, evidently, mere sketches – could be called a metaphysics of the ens or, perhaps more adequately, the metaphysics of the real. And personalism could get along

---

[41] Cf. Zubiri, *Sobre la realidad*, 53.

well with this metaphysics as long as it does not again have the pretension of being a universal categorization of what is real. But even in the case of such a pretension, as occurs with Zubiri's metaphysics, the tensions would be minimized, since this metaphysics would not analyze the different modalities "of being" on the basis of a simplistic analogy, but from the starting point of the different modalities of "the real." And the real not only does not have to be unitary, it actually tends to present itself as not being unitary, particularly if we attend to the person. Thus, from this perspective, the particular ens/thing/res which we call person would demand a specific and peculiar attention, different from the rest; that is, it would demand some specific categories which we have called personalist categories.

Integral Experience as First Epistemology

We are going to close our itinerary with an exposition of the mode of knowledge which Integral Personalism proposes and which we have called integral experience. In reality, it would be possible to close the discourse with the previous chapter, since the vision of the relations between personalism and metaphysics that we have presented falls or stands on its own. Indeed, we may sustain that personalism is first philosophy because it can gain access to the topic of the person directly. But if we are in a condition to make explicit the concrete mode, the *specific gnoseological path*, through which this occurs, the proposal will logically be strengthened. In other words, it is not necessary to have a theory of knowledge in order to sustain personalism's category as first in its area, because it is a fact about which we have evidence and on which personalism has been nourished in constructing its original anthropology. Personalism does not begin with a theory of knowledge. But if it has that theory at hand, the circle closes more perfectly and our presentation of personalism as a first sectorial philosophy becomes stronger. And, since that theory exists, we will present it in what follows, starting with its essential features and, secondly, centering on the aspect that now appears most relevant: its radical epistemological character and the consequences which derive from it.[1]

5.1 Essential Features of Integral Experience

a) Integral Experience

By integral experience we mean the first and direct contact, in a lived way [*de tipo vivencial*], with reality in the widest sense of this word. Therefore, we can define it as *meaningful personal activity*. Activity, because experience is a process; it occurs in action and through action. Personal, because it is experienced by the person, the *entire* person. The complete person is involved in experience:

---

[1] See J. M. Burgos, "Integral experience: a new proposal on the beginning of knowledge," in J. Beauregard, S. Smith (eds.), *In the Sphere of the personal. New perspectives in the philosophy of person* (Wilmington USA Vernon Press, 2016), 41-58. An overall exposition in Juan Manuel Burgos *La Fuente Originaria*. See also Juan Manuel Burgos, *La experiencia integral*. Both texts have as a starting point the ideas expressed very briefly and succinctly by Wojtyła in *Person and Action*.

the body, the senses, the emotions, the intelligence, the heart.[2] It is the human being who experiences and not just the senses, the consciousness or the intelligence; and not even just the self. Finally, experience is meaningful, that is, experience as a phenomenon which is lived out [*vivencial*] has content which is meaningful for the person and which constitutes the basis of the person's knowledge about himself and about the world. In conclusion, we may describe experience as the living and primary confrontation with existence in its meaningful dimension. I live, and by living I experience myself and reality as structures of meaning which conform my existence.

If we take another step and search for its *epistemological* structure, we find two essential features. The first is its double dimension: objective and subjective, which appear simultaneously in the unitary phenomenon of experience. In the words of Karol Wojtyła, "the experience of anything which is found outside the human being always brings with it a certain experience of the human being himself. Because the human being never experiences anything external to himself without, in some way, simultaneously experiencing himself."[3] In each act of experience, in each interaction with reality, these two aspects always become present: the experience of the phenomenon that is external to my subjectivity and the experience of my own subjectivity in experiencing that phenomenon. This complex character allows one to account for the objective and subjective dimensions of knowledge, one of the features which defines the way of understanding human experience as integral experience.

The second decisive feature derives from the consideration that experience is a personal phenomenon, a phenomenon of the entire person, as we said. And, therefore, *intellect and senses act together from the very beginning of the experiential process.* This is the second central epistemological feature of integral experience: *the integration of intellect and sensing in one cognitive act, responsible for the meaningful dimension of experience.* In many epistemological contexts (both realist and non-realist), there is a consideration that in the contact with reality, the senses intervene *first* and, later on, over what is contributed by the senses, intelligence intervenes. This is the thesis of Aristotle and Thomas Aquinas, but also that of Kant, although the interpretation and consequences that each one derives regarding knowledge are very different. But they coincide in this common principle which, however, seems to crash headlong with the reality of knowledge understood as a personal phenomenon. Is it really possible to think that intelligence is incapable of gaining direct access to reality and that it can

---

[2] See von Hildebrand, *The Heart.*

[3] Wojtyła, *Persona y acción*, 31.

only do so through the senses? The theory of integral experience sustains that it is not; it sustains that experience as meaningful is a personal phenomenon and, therefore, intelligence is present *from the beginning* in the cognitive process. In other words, intelligence touches reality.[4] This aspect is decisive in order to be able to sustain the radicality of this cognitive path.

b) Comprehension

The second level in the cognitive process is proportioned by comprehension which should be understood as the *necessary stabilization of experience.* Experience, in effect, is mutable, changing, it never stops nor becomes fixed and, to it, could be applied the famous words of Heraclitus: we can never have the same experience twice. Thus, it is necessary to stabilize it, fix it in place, and set its limits in stable units of meaning which allow us to comprehend in an ordered and relatively constant way the (external and internal) world, the only way, moreover, to make intersubjective communication possible, since individual experience as such can hardly be transmitted. *Comprehending, in conclusion, means transforming lived experience into explicit knowledge;* and, therefore, analyzable, interpretable, expressible, and transmissible knowledge.

The path which leads from experience to comprehension is taken by means of a process of *induction,* not of abstraction, which has been described with precision by Wojtyła in a long text which, due to its interest, we reproduce completely: "It is the task of induction to capture, from the starting point of this multiplicity and complexity of phenomena, its substantial qualitative identity (that is, what we have previously defined as stabilization of the object of experience)." At least Aristotle seems to understand the inductive function of understanding in this way. Modern positivists, J. S. Mill, for example, have a different conception than Aristotle, conceiving induction as a form of argumentation, while for Aristotle it is neither a form of argumentation nor of reasoning; it is the intellectual capturing of the unity of meaning in the multiplicity and complexity of phenomena. Connecting with the previous

---

[4] In this aspect, it is a theory very close to the sentient intelligence of Xavier Zubiri: "Human intelligence is sentient intelligence. [...] Sentient intelligence is not a sensible intelligence, that is, an intelligence poured into what the senses offer it, but rather it is an intelligence which is structurally one with sensing. Human intelligence senses reality. It is not an intelligence that begins by conceiving and judging what it senses. Philosophy has opposed sensing to the activity of the intellect, paying attention only to the content of certain acts. But it has slipped on formality. And it is here that the activity of the intellect and sensing not only are not opposed but, despite their essential irreducibility, constitute one structure, the same structure which, depending on where one looks at it, should be called sentient intelligence or intellective sensing." Zubiri, *Inteligencia y razón,* 351.

commentaries on the experience of the human being, we may say that induction leads the experience of the human being to the simplicity which we observe in that experience despite all its complexity.

"When the experience of the human being takes the form of understanding the person through action, that understanding summarizes in itself all the simplicity of that experience, and it is the expression of that simplicity. Thus, from the perspective of the person's taking on of experience, we have passed from a multiplicity of cases to their qualitative identity; that is, to the recognition that in each one of the cases 'the human being acts,' one finds a 'person-action' relation of the 'same type,' that the same type of person is manifested through action. Qualitative identity which is equivalent to identity of meaning. Reaching this unity is the work of induction; since experience in itself leaves us with a multiplicity of cases. However, in experience all the richness of the phenomena in their diversity constituted by particular individuals remains, while understanding captures the unity of meaning in all of them. In order to capture this unity, the intellect allows itself to be dominated in a certain sense by experience; but, at the same time, without ceasing to comprehend its richness and its diversity (as is sometimes erroneously attributed to abstraction). Thus, for example, when the understanding assumes person and action from the starting point of the experience of the human being, from the starting point of phenomena of the type 'the human being acts,' the understanding remains open in this essential comprehension to all the richness and variety of the data of experience."[5]

What are the essential key ideas of this text?

1. *Induction consolidates and sets a unit of meaning;* it discovers the units of meaning which are made present in the processes of experience, and thus it simplifies experience itself, giving it direction and coherence. The person can structure the variable multiplicity of his facts of experience thanks to these units of meaning.

2. *The units of meaning have a sensible-intellectual content* because they are the result of a process of "consolidation" or "stabilization" which is not reached by the elimination of content (as occurs in abstraction) but by seeking to set the central nucleus which is repeated: the *qualitative identity* which is an identity of meaning and *contains sensible and intellectual elements fused together in the phenomenon which I experience.* That fixing or determination is not necessarily produced by pure repetition of elements, by generalization, or by reasoning, but by *comprehension, by intellection.* I understand that the

---

[5] Wojtyła, *Persona y acción*, 47-48.

realities with which I interact are "trees" or "plants" or "persons." And, in order to do so, I do not need to contemplate a thousand trees or a thousand persons. The assumption of just *one* of them may be enough, because the nucleus of induction does not consist in repetition, but in the ability of my intellect to *comprehend* what or who is before me.[6]

3. *Units of meaning have an objective-subjective content.* Induction does not proceed mainly by way of elimination of content, but by way of the stabilization of experimental content proper to each subject. Thus, units of meaning, in addition to the objective dimension, which is the dimension mainly sought with induction, continue to maintain a certain subjective dimension, which allows one to explain, moreover, why the units of meaning elaborated for different persons will never be exactly identical. The identity will be greater if induction operates on (relatively) simple things, and lesser in complex events or in those in which the subject is more profoundly implicated.

4. *Units of meaning remain open to the variety and richness of the data of experience.* The units of meaning always remain in contact with experience. They are not a *radically* different type of knowledge. They are a consolidation of the original knowledge implicit in experience. They are not experience, in the strict sense, since then they would be fluid and changing; but nor are they an abstract and separate knowledge which, once constituted, never again needs to return to experience. The units of meaning always remit to experience as the configuring matrix of their epistemological validity and as the absolute source of knowledge. Therefore, they remain open to the variety and richness of the data of experience, both in their structural configuration, since they have not been constituted by elimination of the sensible, and due to the attraction which any being has to the source from which it is nourished.

Thus, the individual process should be completed with *the process of exploration of reality in a circular mechanism of coming and going.* Induction stabilizes and objectifies reality (to a certain point), facilitating comprehension. But, by doing so, it establishes a new starting point which remits again to experience. I may,

---

[6] The difference with empiricist induction is that, in the latter, it is not always clear that there is a process of *comprehension* of what is essential, instead of a mere generalization of the data. "Induction [...] may, then, be summarily defined as Generalization from Experience." John Stuart Mill, *A System of Logic* (Toronto: Routledge and Kegan Paul, 1973), 306.

for example, fix a unit of meaning which indicates to me the existence of a type of reality which I call "flower," but once this fact is fixed, the attentive return to experience will show me that this unit of meaning is very wide and not very precise, since there seem to be realities which are significantly different within this unit. With attention, effort, and work, this attitude will lead me to a new process of induction that will seek to set the lesser units of meaning which I find in the initial unit of meaning: roses, carnations, geraniums, etc.

We may, then, consider comprehension as constituted by two processes which self-nourish each other in a circular movement. Through induction, we structure, fix, and simplify experience through the generation of units of meaning which allow us to comprehend it with greater depth. But knowledge calls to knowledge. And the structuring of experience, at the same time that it simplifies it, shows its richness and complexity, soliciting a new exploration in order to contrast data, augment our volume of experience or investigate the possible existence of new units of meaning. And, when this is achieved, entirely or partly, the process is repeated. New experiences generate new inductions, and so on and so forth. But always with the primacy of experience.[7]

c) Critical Comprehension: Science

Critical comprehension constitutes the *third level* of knowledge. It is the process – which is only activated on certain occasions – by which the habitual system of knowledge in persons is transformed *into a critical or scientific knowledge, that is, into a science.* This phenomenon occurs when one attempts to specify in a radical way the validity of knowledge, augment it, consolidate it, etc. It is a very complex process which may acquire many modalities and lead both to the experimental sciences and to philosophy, but which contains in its origin a similar attitude: to seek a knowledge which can be above the errors, imprecisions, or shortcomings which are typical in the common man's cognitive process.

One of the principal features of this process is its *critical* character, meaning by this the need to test all previous knowledge, in such a way that this secondary knowledge is only built on true and consolidated knowledge (to the extent that this is possible). The critical comprehension consists precisely in this, although it operates in a different way in philosophy and in science. It is not necessary to take note here of the essential features of these processes, since the only point that we are now interested in specifying is that the *critical*

---

[7] Other features of comprehension that we will not deal with here are interpretation, notions, truth, return, systematic ordinary knowledge (*saberes*). Cf. Burgos, *La Fuente originaria*, Part. II: Comprehension.

character of science, necessary in order for it to be called a science, does not imply, however, *a radical doubt or questioning of all previous knowledge in a Cartesian way*, because this attitude would imply questioning the validity of experience, which is the unreplaceable source of all knowledge. And, if one radically questions experience, that is, if one doubts about its ability to offer solid and valid knowledge, then knowledge simply self-destructs. The history of epistemology gives us abundant examples of this process, beginning with the very founder of this tendency, Descartes, who had to make recourse to God in order to solve the problems created by methodical doubt.[8] But this recourse is obviously false: it is no more than a flee forward. Knowledge can only be founded on itself. There is no escape route. Either we trust our knowledge radically (which does not mean totally), that is, either we admit that experience can give us the truth about what exists, even though the possibility of error exists (error can only exist to the extent that there is truth) or we annul the possibility of knowing reality. There is no alternative.

In positive terms, what critical comprehension sustains is that *there is an essential continuity between spontaneous knowledge and scientific knowledge or, in our terminology, between comprehension and critical comprehension.* And this continuity exists because both have their origin *in the one and only cognitive ability* of the human being, which can operate with greater or lesser rigor, with more or less information, with better or poorer means, but which, in any case *is always the same*. Therefore, if one admits that, in its initial phases, human cognitive ability is absolutely incapable of offering consolidated truths, there will be no other choice than to conclude that it is incapable of doing so in any other phase. Please understand the thesis. We do not question here, obviously, the possibility of error. What we question is the validity of radical doubt about spontaneous knowledge or experience because, if one sustains this doubt, all knowledge, including scientific knowledge, loses its foundation. Even the most sophisticated scientific investigations depend, in the end, on the ability of human knowledge to read and correctly understand the results of the experiments performed. If we did not trust this ability, the most powerful telescopes and the most sophisticated instruments would be completely useless. What integral experience affirms, in conclusion, is that between comprehension and critical comprehension there is an essential continuity which, of course, must be validated in each *specific* situation.

---

[8] Cf. Edmund Husserl, *Cartesian Meditations* (Springer, 2012) and Paul S. McDonald, *Descartes and Husserl: The Philosophical Project of Radical Beginnings* (Albany: State University of New York Press, 2000).

5.2 A Radical Epistemology

By radicality in epistemology we mean the impossibility of going further, of taking another step in the foundation of reality which could be a final and definitive explanation of the level on which we find ourselves. If this were possible, the knowledge which we have at our disposal at this moment would be a *secondary* knowledge, in contrast to that final (or first) knowledge, which would give the definitive explanation of the events and which, therefore, should be justly called first knowledge or first philosophy.[9]

Now, from all we have said, it is evident that *integral experience is a first and radical knowledge since it is not possible to go beyond it in any sense since there is nothing beyond experience.* Experience, in effect, is not just the principal and first means of access to reality, but the *only one.* And, in order for this aspect to become sufficiently clear and justified we have stressed two fundamental facts of this theory: 1) experience is sensory and intellectual; 2) both comprehension and critical comprehension are derived knowledge.

The fact that experience is sensory and intellectual at the same time, that is, that it contains both dimensions, is decisive in order to be able to affirm its radical character, which would not occur if one affirmed that it is only or primarily sensory (Thomas Aquinas, Hume, Kant). Because, then, who could account for the last or decisive contents of reality? One would have to resort to a source that each theory would justify in a different way – the agent intellect, *a priori* forms, innate ideas – but which, in any case, would imply that part of knowledge *would not proceed from experience* which would invalidate its radical and final character.[10] In the same way, the *continuity* of the process which leads from experience to comprehension and from comprehension to critical comprehension is decisive since, if we do not admit this continuity, we must postulate *two independent starting points of knowledge*, experience being the less radical of them, which would also do away with its primary character. This is what happens in Husserlian phenomenology, when one puts the "natural attitude" in parentheses, that is, one doubts the radical validity of spontaneous knowledge. There is no other solution than to abandon experience, which is just what Husserl does: *"we substitute the concept of*

---

[9] See Chapter 1.2 b: "Metaphysics or First Philosophy as the Epistemologically Ultimate Knowledge."

[10] In the case of Thomism, the agent intellect does not add contents, but it poses a notable difficulty: explaining what the origin of intellectual contents is, if from the beginning only sensory data are possessed. "Oportebat autem ponere aliquam virtutem ex parte intellectus, quae faceret intelligibilia in actu, per abstractionem specierum a conditionibus materialibus. Et haec necessitas ponendi intellectum agentem." Thomas Aquinas, *S. Th.* I, q. 79, a. 3.

experience with the more general one of intuition and therefore we reject the identification between science in general and empirical science."[11]

But, if one maintains the two theses that we sustain, and which we consider to be justified by the analysis of the facts, experience appears in all its original and primordial character: the source from which all knowledge proceeds and the final and first principle of contrasting of knowledge, that is, it appears as an absolutely radical knowledge.

And this is the *epistemologically central fact* which allows *anthropology and ethics to be constituted as first philosophies.* Since anthropology starts with the experience of the human being and ethics with the experience of good and evil[12]; since this experience possesses all the constitutive elements of what is specific to what is human or to morality; and since there is a continuity between this experience and its philosophical formulation, anthropology or ethics only depend, on the most fundamental level, on themselves and on their confrontation with experience. And, therefore, they are first philosophies, although *sectorial* ones. That means that *the totality of experience cannot be encompassed by any science* or, in other words, that human knowledge can only acquire a scientific character if it explores, with a specific methodology, a concrete area of reality, in such a way that it depends on other segments of experience and on its peculiar scientific formalization, in terms of the atom of the web of knowledge. But this dependence is not radical nor structural. If it is a fundamental or first science, like anthropology or ethics, it will depend on others only in an indirect or secondary way, as a complement, completion, or consolidation of what it studies.

In the framework of this epistemological theory, if one sector of philosophy has the pretension, by achieving an overall vision, of thus becoming a metaphysics, it has the right to attempt it, and in light of the results, one will be able to determine what its value is. But that does not at all make it the first science *par excellence,* since *the other areas of knowledge will never radically depend on its results, but rather on the direct analysis of the sector of reality with which they are occupied.* A conclusion which is valid, even if metaphysics sustains that it is occupied with being, that is, with what is most general and present in all of reality, since being is not a primary notion, but a secondary one, which also needs an interpretation and validation. And given reality, what

---

[11] Edmond Husserl, *Ideas relativas a una fenomenología pura y a una filosofía fenomenológica,* J. Gaos, trans. (Madrid: FCE, 1993), 50. The emphasis is ours. English: *Ideas. General Introduction to Pure Phenomenology* (Routledge 2014).

[12] Cf. Karol Wojtyła, "El problema de la experiencia en la ética," in K. Wojtyła, *Mi visión del hombre,* 4th ed. (Madrid: Palabra, 2003), 321-352.

is there, naked reality, which is truly primary, is not, of course, an area exclusive to a possible metaphysics, but an elemental knowledge which a human being possesses through his experience, and which does not need for its structural scientific formulation anything more than the passage to comprehension and to critical comprehension.

Conclusion:
Personalism as a First Philosophy

We wondered, at the start of these pages, if personalism needed another philosophy in order to be an ultimate and radical reflection on the human being. And we wondered, more concretely, about its relationship with metaphysics and its possible condition as a first (or ultimate) area of knowledge. Historically, that function corresponded for many centuries to metaphysics, conceived as the founding, radical, and first area of knowledge on which the other areas of knowledge should necessarily rest; therefore, the rest of the areas of knowledge will be secondary or applied. Modernity did away with this approach, initiating a process of dethroning and destruction of metaphysical knowledge, but the traditional approach, based on the metaphysics of being of Aristotle and Thomas Aquinas, maintained a high degree of relevance in the framework of the classical tradition, into which a good portion of personalism can, to some extent, be integrated. Therefore, our initial question derived into other more contextualized ones: What is the philosophical position of personalism in relation to metaphysics of being? Does personalism need that metaphysics in order to affirm ultimate truths about the human being, and to what extent? Or, on the contrary, is that metaphysics unnecessary for personalism?

We have had to take a relatively long path in order to reach our conclusions. First of all, in order to isolate the problem and not generate equivocations, we had to differentiate four possible meanings of the term metaphysics: metaphysics as an overall area of knowledge; metaphysics as a structural or epistemological first philosophy; metaphysics as a philosophy capable of proportioning absolute knowledge; and metaphysics as metaphysics of being.

Centering on metaphysics of being, a key point in our discourse, we noted that we had to clearly distinguish two realms: the categorial realm, formed by the Aristotelian categories (substance and accidents, potency and act, form and matter), and the transcendental realm, constituted by the level of being and the transcendentals. The first realm has been shown to be decidedly incompatible with personalist anthropology because Aristotelian categorial universality is not adequate for understanding the human being and, if it is used with this objective, the result is a darkening and deformation of what is specifically human. The transcendental realm has been more elusive. While the notions of essence and act of being do not present, in general terms, difficulties for a personalist anthropology, the notion of being has shown a certain tendency toward impersonality in terms of ontotheology, as occurs in the

Heideggerian position and, perhaps, in some versions of the Thomistic position. Therefore, we have proposed a path toward a metaphysics *of the ens or of the real* in Zubirian terms. Something which does not impede that, in our judgment, Thomas Aquinas' proposal on the essence/act of being composition be fundamentally valid and capable of being taken up by personalism and, in particular, by Integral Personalism. But whether one takes up metaphysics of being or another metaphysics like that of Zubiri, we believe we have clearly demonstrated that personalism should never pass necessarily through metaphysical categories. Personalism is essentially self-sufficient for the construction of anthropology and, to that extent, it is a first philosophy.

This is the central nucleus of our conclusions, and it has solid reasons in its favor. First of all, the analysis of the human person may be performed directly: the person is there, to be observed, analyzed, and studied. There is no need for metaphysics in order to begin this analysis. Nor is it necessary in order to arrive at the radical essence of what constitutes the human being. More still, the opposite occurs. If we understand metaphysics as a universal categorization that can be applied to reality, this categorization, limited by its universality, will never be capable of *adequately* comprehending what the human being is. That is the function of anthropology. Therefore, anthropology and, in particular, personalism understood as an anthropology constructed from the starting point of experience is first philosophy.

Now, the fact that personalism is a first philosophy does not mean that it is the *only* first philosophy. From our perspective, any science with the capacity for direct access to its subject matter, as occurs, for example with ethics through moral experience, may be constituted as a first philosophy for the same reasons as anthropology. Therefore, our precise and definitive affirmations would be the following: *anthropology (like social philosophy, ethics or aesthetics) is a first sectorial philosophy capable of establishing ultimate and radical truths about its subject matter.* And, precisely because it is sectorial, the collaboration and relationship with other sciences is welcomed and, in a certain way, necessary. Anthropology is enriched with ethics and social philosophy, and vice versa. But each one of them possesses an ultimate truth about its subject matter because each one of them addresses a sector of reality that is specific and, to some extent, irreducible. The social behavior of the human being cannot be formalized in an essential philosophical anthropology nor is it identical to his ethical behavior. In each one of these realms, there are irreducible elements that require specific studies which respect the complexity and plurality of what exists.

Now, if we affirm anthropology as a sectorial first philosophy – as it seems we should – what mission or role corresponds to the metaphysics of being? As the reader has probably been able to observe through these pages, we have many doubts about the possible validity of a universalistic metaphysics. But, despite that, we consider that this type of analysis can generate elements of comprehension of reality and categorizations that can be employed, duly transformed and adapted, in the personal realms, generating significant illumination. But, we insist, they will never be ultimate categories through which anthropology has to necessarily pass in such a way that they configure its conceptual structure. On the contrary, when it is a question of the human person, metaphysics will have to take into account the results of anthropology and include them in its possible categorization of the whole of reality. A reflection which points toward another possibly valuable contribution of metaphysics: an overall vision of what exists, which anthropology, because it is a sectorial area of knowledge, cannot proportion and which, however, is important in order to insert the human being into the cosmos. This contribution would doubtless be relevant and welcome, but we cannot obviate the difficulty that we note in this project, that is, the difficulty of offering a *scientific* (and not just sapiential) vision of such a multiple and varied set of realities.

These theses are sustained (or fall) by themselves. But they will be corroborated if the *epistemological path* which anthropology follows in order to understand its subject matter, that is, the person, is made explicit. Therefore, we have dedicated the last chapter of the book to presenting the central ideas of integral experience, the epistemological path which, in our opinion, the human mind follows in order to forge its knowledge. The person makes contact with reality through an objective and subjective, intelligent and sensory experience. There everything is given, it is the original source. Anthropology is constructed as the critical comprehension of the content of that source in regards to the human being, a task which does not require permission from any other science. And through that comprehension, it establishes truths that it considers ultimate and radical. The same occurs with ethics, aesthetics or… metaphysics. Metaphysics also has the original source, that is, experience, as its starting point, since there is no other possible beginning. And to the extent that, through the necessary processes of objectification and universalization, it generates valid and suggestive content, it contributes to human knowledge and converges in the construction of philosophy. But it will never be able to tell anthropology what it should or should not sustain about the human person. Because anthropology or, more specifically, every anthropology that wants to begin radically from experience, and therefore integral personalism, is a first philosophy in its own realm.

Bibliography

Alessi, Adriano. *Sui sentieri dell'essere. Introduzione alla metafísica.* 2nd ed. Rome: LAS, 2004.

Alvira, Tomás, Luis Clavell, and Tomás Melendo. *Metafísica.* Pamplona: Eunsa, 1985.

Aristotle. *Metaphysics* by C. D. C. Reeve. Cambridge: Hackett Publishing Company, Inc., 2016.

——. *Categories.*

——. *Topics.*

——. *Nicomachean Ethics.*

Aubenque, Pierre. *El problema del ser en Aristóteles.* Madrid: Escolar y Mayo, 2003.

——. *¿Hay que deconstruir la metafísica?* Madrid: Encuentro, 2009.

——. "Suárez y el advenimiento del concepto de ente." *Logos. Anales del Seminario de Metafísica,* 48 (2015).

von Balthasar, Hans Urs. "Uno sguardo d'insieme sul mio pensiero." *Communio* 105 (1989), 41-42.

Benavides, Christian. "El ser en Tomás de Aquino desde la perspectiva de Cornelio Fabro." *Azafea. Revista filosófica,* 16 (2014), 111-131.

Bengtsson, Jan Olof. *The worldview of personalism.* Oxford: Oxford University Press, 2006.

Beuchot, Mauricio. *Tratado de hermenéutica analógica. Hacia un nuevo modelo de interpretación.* Mexico: UNAM, 2015.

Bowne, Borden P. *Personalism.* Cambridge: The Riverside Press, 1908.

Brock, Stephen L. *Action and Conduct. Thomas Aquinas and the Theory of Action.* Bloomsbury: T& T Clark 1997.

Burgos, Juan Manuel. *La experiencia integral. Un método para el personalismo.* Madrid: Palabra, 2015.

——. "Integral experience: a new proposal on the beginning of knowledge." In *In the Sphere of the personal. New perspectives in the philosophy of person,* edited by J. Beauregard, S. Smith. Wilmington, USA: Vernon Press, 2016, 41-58.

——. "El yo como raíz ontológica de la persona. Reflexiones a partir de John F. Crosby", *Quién* 6 (2017), 33-54.

——. *An Introduction to Personalism.* Washington, DC: CUA Press, 2018.

——. *Repensar la naturaleza humana.* México: Siglo XXI, 2018.

——. *La vía de la experiencia o la salida del laberinto.* Madrid: Rialp, 2018.

——. "Anglo-American and European personalism: A dialogue on idealism and realism". *American Catholic Philosophical Quarterly* 93, 3 (2019), 483-495.

——. "De la sustancia al yo como fundamento de la persona." *Quién* 10 (2019), 27-44.

——. "Wojtyła's Personalism as Integral Personalism. The future of an Intellectual Project", *Questionaes Disputatae* 9, 2 (2019).

——. *Personalist Anthropology: a philosophical guide to life*. Vernon Press: Wilmington, 2022.

——. *La Fuente originaria. Una teoría del conocimiento*. Granada: Comares 2023.

Calvo, Tomás. *Introducción a la Metafísica de Aristóteles*. Gredos, Madrid 2014.

Caputo, John D. *Heidegger and Aquinas: An Essay on Overcoming Metaphysics*. New York: Fordham University Press, 2003.

Clavell, Luis and Miguel Pérez de Laborda. *Metafísica*. Rome: Edusc, 2006.

Crosby, John F. *The Personalism of John Paul II*. Steubenville: Hildebrand Press, 2019.

——. "On solitude, subjectivity and substantiality. Response to Juan Manuel Burgos." *Quién* 8 (2018), 7-18.

Díaz, Rafael. "La analogía." In *Philosophica: Enciclopedia filosófica online*, edited by Francisco Fernández Labastida and Juan Andrés Mercado. URL: <http://www.philosophica.info/archivo/2010/voces/analogia/Analogia.html>

Fabro, Cornelio. *Participación y casualidad según Tomás de Aquino*. Pamplona: Eunsa, 2009.

Florido, Francisco León. "Estudio preliminar de Francisco Suárez, Disputaciones metafísicas." Madrid: Tecnos, 2011, 38-43.

Forment, Eudaldo. *Ser y persona*. 2nd ed. Barcelona: Ediciones de la Universidad de Barcelona, 1983.

Gilson, Étienne. *Being and some philosophers*. 2nd edition. Toronto: Pontifical Institute of Mediaeval Studies, 1952.

González Álvarez, Ángel. *Tratado de Metafísica I. Ontología*. 2nd ed. (Madrid: Gredos, 1967).

Groarke, Louis. *An Aristotelian Account of Induction. Creating Something from Nothing*. Montreal: McGill-Queen's University Press, 2009.

Heidegger Martin. *Die onto-theologische Verfassung der Metaphysik, in Identität und Differenz*. Pfullingen, 1957.

——. *Being and Time*. Harper Collins, 2008.

von Hildebrand, Dietrich. *The Heart*. South Bend, IN: St. Augustine's Press, 2007.

Holub, Grzegorz. *Understanding the Person. Essays on the Personalism of Karol Wojtyła*. Berlin-New York: Peter Lang, 2021.

Husserl, Edmund. *Cartesian Meditations*. Springer 2012.

——. *Ideas. General Introduction to Pure Phenomenology*. Routledge 2014.

Levinas, Emmanuel. *Totality and Infinity: An Essay on Exteriority*. Pittsburgh, PA: Duquesne University Press, 1969.

——. *De la existencia al existente*. Madrid: Arena Libros, 2006.

Llach, Gonzalo. "Heidegger y su interpretación del esse tomista." *Aporía* 6 (2013), 47-58

Lyotard, Jean-François. *The postmodern condition. A report on knowledge*. Manchester University Press: Manchester, 1984.

Marías, Julián. *Idea de la metafísica*. Madrid: Editorial Columba, 1962.

——. *Metaphysical Anthropology: The Empirical Structure of Human Life*. University Park, PA: Pennsylvania State University Press, 1971.

Marion, Jean-Luc. *God without Being*. Chicago: University of Chicago Press, 2012.

McDonald, Paul S. *Descartes and Husserl: The Philosophical Project of Radical Beginnings*. Albany: State University of New York Press, 2000.

Mill, John Stuart. *A System of Logic*, Toronto: Routledge and Kegan Paul, 1973.

Millán-Puelles, Antonio. *Fundamentos de filosofía*. 10th ed. Madrid: Rialp, 1978.

Mounier, Emmanuel. *Personalism*. London: Routledge and Kegan Paul, 1952.

Mortensen, Jonas Norgaard. *The Common Good. An introduction to personalism.* Wilmington: Vernon Press, 2017.

Newman, John Henry. *Essay on the Development of Christian Doctrine*. London: J. Toovey, 1845.

John Paul II. "Fides et Radio." In *Acta Apostolicae Sedis* 90 (1998), 715-788.

Ortega y Gasset, José. *What is philosophy*, W. W. Norton & Company, 1964.

Polo, Leonardo. *Antropología trascendental. I. La persona humana*. Pamplona: Eunsa, 1999.

Possenti, Vittorio. *Ritorno all'essere. Addio alla metafisica moderna.* Rome: Armando Editore, 2019.

Ratzinger, Joseph. *Introduction to Christianity*. Ignatius Press: San Francisco, 2004.

Rhonheimer, Martin. "Ragione pratica e verità della soggettività: l'autoesperienza del soggetto morale alle radici della metafisica e della antropologia." In *Ripensare la metafisica*, edited by L. Romera. Rome: Armando, 2005.

Romera, Luis, ed. *Ripensare la metafisica*. Rome: Armando, 2005.

Rovira, Rogelio. "¿Una lista desordenada y defectuosa? Consideraciones sobre la crítica de Kant al elenco aristotélico de las categorías." *Anuario Filosófico* 39/3 (2006), 747-767.

Thomas Aquinas, *Summa Theologiae*.

——. *Quaestiones Disputatae de Veritate*.

——. *In XII libros Metaphysicorum expositio*.

——. *Commentary on Aristotle's Physics*.

——. *In Iv Libros Sententiarum*.

——. *Expositio super librum Boethii De trinitate*.

——. *Quaestiones Disputatae de Potentia Dei*.

——. *In librum de causis expositio*.

——. *El orden del ser. Antología esencial* (coord. E. Forment) (Madrid: Tecnos, 2003).

Seifert, Josef. *Essere e persona. Verso una Fondazione fenomenologica de una metafisica classica e personalistica*. Milan: Vita e Pensiero, 1989.

——. *Erkenntnis der Vollkommenen. Wege der Vernunft zu Gott*. Rückersdorf: Lepanto Verlag, 2010.

Suárez, Francisco. *Disputationes metafísicas*. Madrid: Ed. Tecnos, 2011.

Wojtyła, Karol. "The Transcendence of the Person in Action and Man's Self-Teleology." In *The Teleologies in Husserlian Phenomenology*, edited by A.T. Tymieniecka. Analecta Husserliana, 1979.

——. "El problema de la experiencia en la ética." In K. Wojtyła, *Mi visión del hombre,*4th ed. Madrid: Palabra, 2003.

——. "La subjetividad y lo irreductible en el hombre." In Karol Wojtyła, *El hombre y su destino.* Madrid: Palabra, 2005, 25-39.

——. *Person and Act and Related Essays.* Washington: Catholic University of America Press, 2021.

Wolff, Christian. *Philosophia prima sive ontologia methodo scientifica pertractata, qua omnis coghnitionis humane principia continentur,* Veronae, MDCCXXXVI, Typis Dionysii Ramanzini Bibliopolae apud S. Thoman.

Zubiri, Xavier. *Los problemas fundamentales de la metafísica occidental.* Madrid: Alianza Editorial, 1994.

——. *Sobre la realidad.* Madrid: Alianza Editorial, 2001.

——. *Inteligencia y razón.* Madrid, Alianza Editorial, 2008.

www.ingramcontent.com/pod-product-compliance
Lightning Source LLC
Chambersburg PA
CBHW050538270326
41926CB00015B/3283